The
Success Ethic
and the
Shattered American
Dream

Benj Franklin

The Success Ethic
and the
Shattered American Dream

Blaine Taylor

A

PUBLISHED BY ACROPOLIS BOOKS LTD. ● WASHINGTON, D.C. 20009

ACROPOLIS BOOKS LTD.
Colortone Building, 2400 17th St., N.W.
Washington, D.C. 20009

Printed in the United States of America by
COLORTONE PRESS, Creative Graphics Inc.
Washington, D.C. 20009

Library of Congress Cataloging in Publication Data

Taylor, Blaine, 1933—
    The success ethic and the shattered American dream.

    Bibliography: p.
    Includes index.
    1. United States — Economic conditions — 1971 —
2. United States — Moral conditions. 3. United States —
Civilization — 20th century. I. Title.
HC106.7.T88   973.925   76-20268
ISBN 0-8749-387-X
ISBN 0-87491-039-0 pbk.

Title page: Ben Franklin was typical of many of the first culture's leading citizens. A generalist who tried to integrate all facets of his world.

Foreword

Let's face it. The American Dream has indeed been shattered. The nation must face up to that fact. An entire people had once been on fire, alive to the possibilities of freedom in an abundant land. For many Americans, who once considered themselves patriots, the fire has gone out, leaving only ashes in their hearts.

Although the American Dream has been shattered, it is not beyond recall. Americans must reclaim, not events, but ideas. Enduring values, not battles, must be celebrated. We must rekindle those beliefs and thoughts which constituted the original American dream. The purpose of this book is to help put that dream together again—to make a beginning in the task of determining and reclaiming basic American values.

The American dream must be redefined for what it really is—the nation's early values and aspirations. Americans must realize that the Villain who has been "doing in" that Dream is the mechanical age, with its shabby and shoddy values.

The mechanical age, without anybody taking much notice of it, has for a long time been foisting on the American people values that are without promise. The need is for some guidelines to smoke out, select, and define basic values. These guidelines can be found in the nation's history. Although the nation has lost its way and has forgotten where it is going, the essentials for gaining a new direction are available to anyone taking the time to look. The necessary wisdom can be found in the American heritage. The past remains prelude to the future and the present, and it's high time Americans dug into their past for what they need at this moment in history.

Today, Americans have arrived in the electronic age—and, of course, they're shook up by it. They are confused because they have been weakened, frightened, and had their sense of values twisted and distorted by the mechanical age.

But they wouldn't be shook up if they realized that the electronic age in which they have arrived could be a Promised Land. And all the electronic age needs to revive the image of the Promised Land is the spiritual, ethical, and work values of the first American culture, for there, indeed, is the foundation for the American Dream.

The first step is to have a look at what's gone before, in the nation's journey to this electronic age, to examine the principles on which the country was built, and find out how and where they were lost. And the next step is to find out why in the mechanical age, which has sandwiched itself between the first culture and this electronic age, Americans have been diverted from those early values, have been led astray, confused, taken . . . to the point where most of the nation today doesn't even know it can have a Promised Land in this electronic age.

And that is what this book is about to do—take those first two steps.

But any subsequent moves toward getting those early values back into the nation's lifestyle is beyond this book. It is the responsibility of every American— young and old, and in between.

For these early values are the American Dream.

Contents

FOREWORD/ 5

PART I
What's Happened to the American Economy?

In a Confused Hangup/13
Roots of American Abundance/14
A Heaven and Money Combination/15
The Puritan Work Ethic/17
Corruption of the Work Ethic Begins/19
Speculators Make Millions/20
The Boss—An Impersonal Abstraction/21
The Young Turned Off/24
Natural Resources are Providentially Provided/25
The Capitalists Destroyed Capitalism/27
The Miracles of Modern Life/28
An Outhouse in Mid-Winter/29
Whale of an Oil Difference/30
Mechanical Age Stopped Mobility/32
One Letter Cost a Day's Pay/33
Today the Inn has Changed/34
A Family Centered Lifestyle/35
Nature Seen as Enemy/36
The Farmer's Life Had Meaning/37
From Industrial to Service Economy/38
Personal Dependence Upon Integrity and Ethics/39
Old Fashioned Virtues/40
Legislation to Rig the Market/41
The Demon of Specialized Slaves/43
Vested Interests Take Over/44
Harbingers of Reclamation of First Culture/46

PART II
Is the Nation's Lifestyle Collapsing?

Uncertainty in a Go-Getter Morality/49
Infiltrated by Success Ethics/50
The Safety Valve of the West/52
Democracy in Puritan Tradition/54
Means to Extend Liberty and Equality/56
Change Hard to Effect/58
Picture of a God Who Cares/60
Grace in the Humble/61

PART III
Is American Culture Crumbling?

A Culture Attracted to the Wild/63
The Puritan as Artist/64
The Individual Made Music/66
The Lonely Colonists Loved Music/67
A Lively Village Culture/68
Pumpkin Yellow Buildings/69
Poor Furniture Didn't Survive/71
The Wonder of New Shapes/73
The American Eagle, Bird of Many Parts/74
Art a Secular Concern/75
Also Some of the Worst Painting/76
West's Mythological Paintings/77
American Folk Art In the Vanguard/79
The American Impressionists/81
Hicks Had the Free Gift of Grace/83
Historian-Painter of Indian Tribes/84
The Literature of an Abundant Land/85
Poe Challenges the Mechanical Age/86
Rich Background in New England History/88
A Veil on Every Face/90
A Hundred Years Before Camus/90
Life in a Whaling Venture/92
The Soul and the Machine/94

Emerson's Leap Into Escapism/95
Thoreau—Child of the First Culture/97
Alone at Walden Pond/98
Sentimental Nothingness/99
All Wood With Some Stain/100
Urban Center No Cultural Bank/101
Tyrannized By Critics/102
Land the Mysterious Consuming Force/103

PART IV
What Is It All About?

God Quietly Retired/105
"Scramble for Bigger Farms?"/107
Puritan Theology Was Good News/108
The Puritan No Militant Predestinarian/110
Augustinian Heritage/112
Seriousness to the Sabbath/113
A Spiritual Basis For a Secular Culture/115
Choose For Or Against God/116
A Full Blown Transcendentalism/117
Winning The West For Christ/118
Attack On Puritan Inheritance/120
Slogans Replace Faith/122
Extremes Dominant in Media/124
The Heritage of Rome/124
The American Way of Life Deified/126
Greatness of Hebrew Covenant Community/127
Christ Bottled and Labeled/127
Clings Fast to Previous Period/129
No Naive Greening of America/130
The New Day/131
American Dreams Come True/132

SUGGESTIONS FOR FURTHER READING/135

INDEX/137

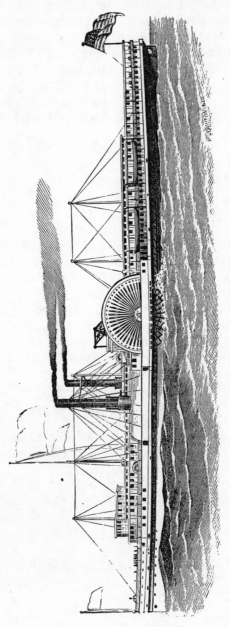

A HUDSON RIVER STEAMBOAT.

The railroad and the river steamboats opened the west, transforming American life. Now central industrial and distribution centers were possible. The Mechanical Age became inevitable.

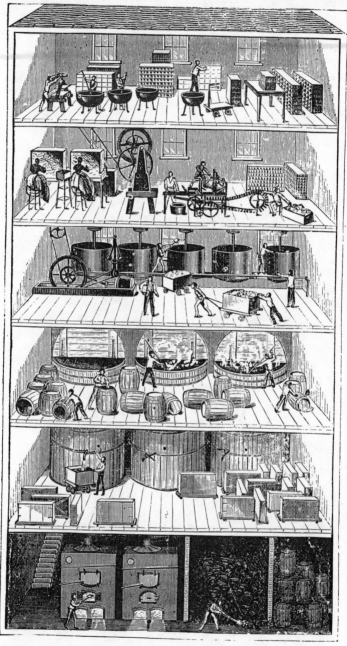

"Soap Manufactory of E. Morgan's Sons" whole families were taken into factories. Lives that had been relatively independent became subject to the decisions of others. Work that had been varied and interesting now became repetitious and boring.

What's Happened to the American Economy?

In a Confused Hangup

The confusion in the nation today can be compared to the frustrations of a small dog who lived during the Second World War.

Four American fliers, stationed in England, had for their mascot a dog that developed a craving for ice cubes. They were his toys—endlessly fascinating and thirst quenching also. More than that, the ice cubes seemed to come alive when he played with them. The dog went crazy if the fliers gave him three or four ice cubes at one time. Instinctively he prepared for the future, and tried to prolong his pleasure by digging a hole in the ground so the ice cubes might be safely buried. Later, perhaps even on another day, he would return to paw, sniff, and dig in a vain effort to reclaim the ice cubes which were no longer there. This gave the fliers continuous entertainment, for it seemed to them delightfully funny and ridiculous.

Today, Americans make the same kind of futile efforts to provide for future security. They also seem unable to learn from experience. And the tragedy is that most now seem to accept, as irredeemable fact, that no matter how long the search, nothing of value will be found. So, frequently disillusioned, most

Americans have developed attitudes of indifference and cynicism. They doubt not only religious doctrines, but the existence of any truth at all. Things continually happen in life, but nothing that happens appears to have purpose or meaning beyond the moment.

All values once taken for granted are now challenged. Even those telling others to be good don't seem at all sure what good is. Fearful that their own spiritual traditions are bankrupt, many frantically search the world like the little dog searching for what has been lost. They rush about spiritually, mentally, philosophically, physically, trying to find guidance in the mysticism of the East, in the polytheism of the past, in the movement of the stars, in a pharmaceutical trip, in anything.

But that doesn't mean there are no values, that there is no good, nothing to hang on to. Values can be found right where the nation is—in the realities of this age, and in the nation's heritage. All Americans need to do is to take a good look at what they have in the religious and philosophical attics, barns and cellars of their nation's yesterdays. From that heritage, they can select what is usable and of value, and they'll find they no longer have the little dog's frustrations, but something really good—a solid reason for being.

Roots of American Abundance

The underlying principles of the American economy are so taken for granted that few people have the foggiest notion how the nation arrived at those principles.

In our beginnings, four factors were so obviously part of the traditions of Christianity and Judaism that they were accepted by a whole people, even skeptics, deists, and free thinkers. Taken together they provided the discipline, the motivation, the rules, the purpose, and the perspective, which made the American economy the strongest the world has ever known.

As long as these factors were genuinely part of the fabric of American life, the economy was able to move through periods of depression, inflation, war and industrial strife, with only short pauses, followed by continuing advances. Perfectly tuned to the natural abundance of the land, these spiritual factors provided the frame for American wealth and power. Today it is not surprising that the nation's most serious economic crisis has come in a time frame immediately following the erosion of these ideals.

American abundance was a result of the nearly universal acceptance of the following religious ideals:

—the Puritan work ethic
—providentially provided natural resources
—a family-centered lifestyle
—personal dependence on integrity and ethics

For almost three hundred years, these four principles provided the prime driving force of the American economy. They have always been challenged by intellectuals, but at the same time have been taken for granted by the general population. Then something began to happen to that driving force to the point that by 1950, a majority of Americans had lost faith in these assumptions. As that skepticism became more universal, the economy experienced from its roots up a more fundamental debilitation. It is time to re-examine the development of these principles, their erosion, and the present and future consequences of that erosion.

A Heaven and Money Combination

An earthly mixture of religious and financial concerns marked the teachings of the Puritan leaders. In return for dedication and discipline, their covenant

15

with God led them to expect rewards in this world and salvation in eternity. The benefits of the good life were to be realized in heaven, but also in the blessings of this world. Private property was taken for granted by the Puritans—an astounding and practically unprecendented assumption. Most came to these shores not for religious liberty, but for a better economic life. Even the spirtually motivated had learned Calvin's lesson, that "to work is to pray." They glorified their efforts by establishing a "vocation." They lost themselves and found themselves in work.

The early settlers discovered a providential land as they cleared the forests, removed the stones and stumps, built the homes and barns, constructed the roads and bridges, cultivated the fields, established commerce, and found natural resources. Throughout the first period, labor was scarce and expensive, land cheap and abundant. More than any other fact, this condition shaped the American economy and culture. During the colonial period any European laborer could double his income by immigration to America. In the abundant land, hard work brought a form of wealth to almost everyone. It is no wonder a work ethic developed.

The first sermon, preached in America in 1621 by Robert Cushman, was called "Self Love." It proclaimed all of God's creation as productively useful, given by providence as the inheritance of mankind, and as a reward for good service. This built the foundation for a philosophy of property rights, which has prevailed in America over any corresponding doctrine of human or civil rights.

As the colonists gained permanence and security in their new land, the quality of life open to them greatly surpassed that available to ordinary individuals anywhere else in the world. Although few settlers were economically wealthy, almost all lived very well. A large majority had land, buildings, and private possessions. Essentially their villages were politically autonomous. Christianity gave goals in life to everybody, and offered salvation to those interested in a hereafter. Since cities were economically unnecessary in the days of home production, people could choose their neighbors for their value as friends and could easily move on if the choice had been unwise. Most of all, life was filled with hope and great expectations, and the colonists naturally found more meaning and purpose.

Time was measured more by the seasons than by days and hours. As they controlled their occupations, people also controlled their time. Almost all worked very hard, but their labor provided a sense of worth; for, with land and materials cheap, work eventually established wealth. In less than five years, a family could clear away the fifteen acres or so it needed to support itself and provide a modest surplus. Freedom from outside economic domination had never been available so cheaply in the history of the world.

The great quality of the first culture and the practical foundation of the Puritan ethic was the fact that in those years, hard work, frugal habits, and cooperative activity did result in legitimate accomplishment, personal possessions, and modest wealth. This gave all involved a positive identity, and a continuing purpose of individual, family and community betterment.

The Puritan Work Ethic

The Puritan work ethic, now so widely ridiculed, has been a great positive force in American history. Its application meant, for the first time in history, that an individual might by personal effort attain economic security and self-realization. While Puritanism decried wasteful expenditure, worldly pleasure, and all forms of indulgence which dissipated either wealth or energy, it did give supreme value to the time and talents of the individual. Previously, apart from the nobility and talented persons under their

17

protection the individual had little value or importance. Puritanism cultivated a system which allowed the individual to take pride in self. Every Christian was called upon to make the most of his life, not only of his skills and possessions, but to perfect his character as well. This developed the spirit of enterprise and industry which made modern capitalism work. Frugality and strong family life encouraged thrift and the accumulation of capital. The careful use of time and talent helped form the regular habits and skills upon which the conduct of industry depends. The emphasis on personal responsibility made every individual feel self-important and involved in the total task. The Puritan work ethic enabled the common person to own private property, to have a pride in individual accomplishment, to be important in the life of the entire community, and to have the hope of an unlimited future. The great spaciousness of America—the availability of land and the assurance that as the consequence of hard work, time would bring inevitable success—deeply affected the nation's thinking. For the first time in the history of the world, the emotional impact of such security was available to the common man. He knew the pride and the responsibility of ownership.

Frederick Jackson Turner, in an impressive and suggestive thesis now substantially challenged, explained this process of American development by viewing the advancing frontier as a "safety valve," which preserved and shaped the form and spirit of American democracy. He felt that free land embodied and preserved the original hopes of the settlers for the pursuit of happiness.

While some scholars argue that Turner was overly romantic in the spirit of his time, and was misled by "the agrarian myth," the West was indeed very influential in preserving the values of early America. Its practical affirmation of democracy added much to the heritage of the nation. And the greatest factor in

the West's contribution to that heritage was cooperation. It was people pulling together which won the
West—riding on wagon trains, building railroads, culti-
vating fields, forming communities, and shaping the
future of those communities. The West also preserved
for years the participant culture of the broad range of
the nation's beginnings. And to the Anglo-Saxon
roots of the East, the West added something new and
exciting—a rich Spanish and French heritage. At the
same time the expansion to the West preserved and
enhanced the values of the first colonial culture.

Corruption of the Work Ethic Begins

Ironically, however, in that American push to the
West, were the seeds that were later to corrupt the
Puritan work ethic. The availability of land led to its
wasteful use. Its abundance led to speculation and
quick profits. The great fortunes which provided the
capital for the mechanical age came largely from land
speculation, not from hard work. Even in New England, before 1775, vast tracts of land were bought
and sold for profit by speculators. Companies for
speculation were formed in great number between
1763 and 1767. Their success eroded much of the
simple faith in hard work, so pervasive in the first
culture. Speculation was a thousand times more pro-
fitable than any form of skilled labor or professional
talent. With profits came power. The Ordinance of
1787, typical of most legislation which followed, gave
further advantage to speculators. Suddenly all voters
had to have not only personal property, but at least
50 acres of land. Candidates for the legislature had to
have at least 200 acres. Soon, great political give-
aways eliminated cheap land. The whole system of
land-grants and homesteads were advertised as free
gifts of a grateful nation to the poor and hardwork-
ing. At best, they turned out to be a way for a few

thousand individuals to absorb a majority share in the total wealth of the nation. Or, more realistically, the land grants were the first instance of a great many frauds engineered by the wealthy and politically powerful. In less than a quarter of a century more than 521,000,000 acres were "surrendered" to the speculators.

Speculators Make Millions

The economic system began to crumble when speculative profit failed to be matched by real risk or real work. Through political power and corruption, the risk was nullified and the profit assured. It was not capitalism and free enterprise that failed. As long as the system was uncorrupted by a pattern of dishonesty, it worked. Success suddenly depended not upon free enterprise at all, but upon government intervention, protection and grants. Often those who did the work, or had the ideas, failed to receive either credit or reward. Whitney, Goodyear, Howe, and hundreds of other inventors struggled with poverty, while speculators made millions on their creations.

Following the lead of the land speculators, business and industry embraced the new golden calf of progress. The work ethic, which the Puritan developed for the glorification of God, was now channeled into a glorification of the speculative system itself. Profits replaced providence in motivation, while ethical and moral concerns became "impractical."

The change was spiritual as well. As purely quantitative success was achieved, it proved to be hollow. Suddenly, conformity became the first essential in behavior. This period, Channing announced, was one which "crushed individuality of judgment and action." It "abolished freedoms" taken for granted in the first culture.

As industry grew, all personal contact between capitalist and worker was eliminated. This made it possible for personally admirable and moral individuals to treat great masses of workers as impersonal machines. In a process so well described by Reinhold Niebuhr, moral men created an immoral society. No longer was there any close relationship between the owner and his employees. They did not even know one another.

The Boss—An Impersonal Abstraction

The growth of corporations also diffused ownership among many stockholders, interested primarily in profits and growth. Control itself was removed from the owners, and put into the hands of businessmen and bankers who judged an enterprise by profitability alone. Suddenly all relationships became utterly impersonal. No longer could the employee seek out the "boss" and talk about his problems. The "boss" was an impersonal abstraction that was blamed for conditions. No longer could the owner oversee what was going on and take a humane interest in his employees.

Even the job itself became so complex that many of the advantages of the work ethic no longer applied. In many jobs, workers had nothing to do with finished products that needed no craftsmanship, had no security, and no one seemed to care about the quality of their work. This left them with neither property, nor pride of accomplishment.

Pig iron, coal, and other metals were mined in the 18th century. After 1800, they fed the industrial revolution.

Before the Revolutionary War there were but two steam engines in the thirteen colonies. One was at a Passaic, New Jersey, copper mine. The other was in a Philadelphia distillery.

Before 1825, seven major technological innovations had transformed the country:

(1) The smooth and continuous production line

made possible by the endless belt, coupled with many different types of converters, made the specialization of work possible and allowed unskilled labor to perform minute portions of work previously reserved for highly skilled craftsmen. Oliver Evans, before 1800, completed construction of a mill in which grain was milled by continuous process without the help of human hands, except at the beginning and end.

(2) Eli Whitney's cotton gin not only unified the South by giving it a new source of wealth, but it created standardization in industry.

(3) Slater's importation of English textile machinery to New England initiated the principle of grouping workers at a central place rather than jobbing out the work.

(4) Fitch's steamboat, popularized by Livingston and Fulton, gave centrally located factories a means of distribution.

(5) Whitney introduced the principle of machine-made, matching interchangeable parts when he agreed to manufacture ten thousand muskets within two years. He achieved the impossible in a country of few expert gunsmiths by substituting "correct and effective operations of machinery for the skill of the artist."

(6) The process of prefabrication was introduced in the building of bridges and homes. All sizes and lengths of building materials were prefitted for on the spot assembly. The European system of riveted lattice construction of bridges was both slow and expensive.

(7) The assembly line, which used a mechanical conveyance to bring the job to workmen at fixed stations, was powered by steam and water, sources of energy which did not tire. This allowed continuous production, with

laborers working in shifts, constantly kept busy by the rhythm and speed of the machines.

These changes were so fundamental that they affected the psychological well being of the American worker. Whole families were taken into factories. Lives that had been relatively independent became subject to the decisions of others. Work that had been varied and interesting now became repetitious and boring.

Families lost their structure by working in the factory environment. Child labor initiated a process, which neither motivated, prepared nor conditioned children for life away from the factory. The twelve to fourteen hours spent at work were so exhausting and dehumanizing, as to prevent even an interest in culture. The wide horizons and ideals of the first culture were lost with hardly a trace. The women ineffectively tried to form associations for education and cultural pursuits, but their heroic attempts were in vain, affecting less than four per cent of all female factory workers.

The literary figures of the day gave support to the newly formed labor movement. Some workers grouped together in an attempt to obtain fair working conditions, decent pay, shorter hours, and time off for recreation. Without notable results, Bryant, Hawthorne, Emerson, Bancroft, and Whitman all fought for the common worker.

The white slavery of the North was almost as evil as the black slavery of the South. Forced to live under such conditions, a whole generation of Americans, black and white, developed a lifestyle about which we have few records and no commentary. The average wage paid to cotton millhands from 1820 to 1830 was forty-four cents a day. By 1850, it had increased to almost a dollar a day. The working day ranged from twelve to fourteen hours long, depending upon the season of the year, and the length of the daylight.

This discipline and diligence of the work ethic were lost. Work became simply a way to survive, a way to get money. It lost its inherent value. No longer was it a calling performed for the glory of God. A direct relationship between the work done and a finished product was harder and harder to perceive. The worth of the individual contribution was often impossible to ascertain. At the same time, injustice and dehumanizing conditions were very easy to see.

The Young Turned Off

By the 1960's, a massive withdrawal of college students from involvement in business and industry had taken place. The best students seemed to want nothing to do with the system. Some romantically "opted out," in a naive and predictable attempt to go "back to the land," to join various communes, and to explore a general "greening of America." Others "turned off" tried to escape through drugs, sex, and music, into a separate culture. Almost all were appalled by the war in Vietnam, racial injustice, and economic privilege amid poverty and human suffering. Although their solutions were less than effective, they represented a general frustration with, and rejection of, the standards and values of the mechanical age. In the 1970's, the Watergate scandal, the energy crisis, general shortages of vital materials and foodstuffs, and continuing international anarchy, brought the frustrations of the young to the majority of the American people. The ineffectiveness of big government and the willingness of big business to profit from crisis invited criticism of all bureaucratic bigness.

Probably an attempt to go back to the soil was inevitable in a society where all the myths and images of success involve the abundant land. The fact that money became the great symbol of success and replaced land as the one measure of intelligence and power, was part of the frustration. Suddenly everything was infinitely quantifiable. A singular preoccupation with quantity was the leading cultural fact of the mechanical age. Everything had to be not only biggest and best, but also most popular and most beautiful.

Work, and the work ethic, were rejected not because work could no longer sustain self-realization, but because the fruits of work were so spiritually debilitating. Material success seemed to cause at least as much misery as it solved. In response to the cry that there must be something more, society neglected to look to the process itself as a means of fulfillment. When work becomes service, a means to understanding, a vehicle for craftsmanship and artistic achievement, a way to solve society's problems, and to enhance and develop family relationships, then the work ethic begins to be understood. Some Americans are beginning to comprehend how important it is to be really needed—to have a job that truly needs to be done, and the ability to do it. Some are beginning to understand the difference between earning a paycheck and having a job that accomplishes something important for others.

Natural Resources Are Providentially Provided

Faith in a benevolent God, a fundamental belief of both Judaism and Christianity, was the shared experience of the first culture. Despite devastating hardships, God would ultimately give the faithful all they needed to prosper. Today's shared experience of contemporary culture is that God, if He exists at all, gives little attention to the least of the brethren. War is everywhere. Millions are starving. Natural resources are being exhausted. The land itself is polluted. Rather than providentially providing for life, the land appears to be systematically raped, yet is not sufficient to sustain either its current population, or the billions yet unborn.

The Puritans believed that God cared for his creatures—all of them—giving them the benefit of His supervision, and ordering all things for their good. Although both the Old and New Testaments are dominated by the thought of Divine Providence, the Puritans found explicit support in the teaching of Jesus in the Sermon on the Mount. He presents a caring Father in whom all may trust. God does not even allow a sparrow to fall to the ground apart from His care. The Lord's Prayer is addressed to one who cares for the bodies and souls of all his children. While the Father is impartial "under a reign of law," he does make a special response to the believing prayer of true disciples (Mark 9:23; 11:22-24). The theological and moral problems of a doctrine of providence are seen to be superseded in the light of the grace and the glory, which shines into the world because of Easter. They took literally the injunction: "I am God Almighty: be fruitful and multiply; a nation and a company of nations shall come from you." (Genesis 35:11).

Although the struggle was real, the combination of hard work and the abundant land gave confirmation to the doctrine. But ironically, its successful application led to disillusionment. The abundant land was stripped for quick profits because it was so rich and plentiful. Ambition turned into conspicuous consumption because all goals had become exclusively quantitative. At the same time free enterprise and economic independence for all individuals became a threat to the powerful, as soon as they themselves had achieved financial success. It was the successful speculators who first called for government interference. They wanted protective tariffs, grants of land and money, price support and stabilization, government contracts, regulation and legislation. They wanted these to protect their vested interests, to give them favorable tax policies, to enable them to control markets and labor.

The Capitalists Destroyed Capitalism

The self-professed capitalists destroyed capitalism in America. It was their political manipulation which first contributed to the destruction of the natural resources of the abundant land. Every major national resource was first discovered and developed in the atmosphere of free enterprise. All were exploited in the same way. Then the free economy was compromised by government intervention. Most of the profits, and almost all government grants, went to the speculators. Very little was retained for conservation of resources, for experimentation and research; none at all for fighting pollution. The powers of government were consistently used to serve the profits possible through waste, duplication and pollution. The cotton and tobacco planter could make more money if he didn't rotate his crops. The lumberman became wealthy by moving on to level new areas, creating more wasteland instead of preparing to use again land already raped. The railroads found far more money and land available through duplication of lines, than through cooperation. Miners could gain larger returns by stripping the land. Privileges granted by government, by the nature of the bureaucratic process, point always to the past, protecting what is, not what should be.

While operative, the belief in providence elicited two responses, both vital for the national economy. One was the attitude of thankful stewardship toward what God had given. The other was an attitude of creative innovation in response to challenge, in order to find nature's solution. These attitudes still furnish the one key which could open the medicine cabinet to cure the economic ills in America. Anything less— especially the whining self-pity now so common—

simply won't do it. The nation will never solve the problems of inflation, of recession and unemployment, of older people on fixed incomes, and of taxation, without these twin attitudes of thankfulness and creativity.

The Miracles of Modern Life

First of all—what do Americans have to be thankful for? What has God given them for which they may feel a thankful stewardship? For one thing—the miracles of modern life. Almost every American has a transistor radio, record player, and a stereophonic tape recorder. Many still alive can remember when only a handful of people had ever heard an orchestra play. If one loved classical music, even if money and time were available, it would take a three or four-day trip, and an extraordinary coincidence, to hear a concert. Today neither time nor space is a problem. Music, news, and every variety of cultural input is constantly available.

Almost everyone has a camera. One hundred years ago, not even the richest king could look at the pictures of his children and of his grandchildren, and relive the past highlights of his life with clear images memory had dimmed or forgotten. Through photography, any modern man—not only the richest king—may recall events, and repeat trips he has taken in the years before.

Also the great art books—"Museums Without Walls" Andre Malraux calls them—bring the world's masterpieces into every home. In the age of the paperback book revolution, anyone may have on his own bookshelves for a week's pay, all the classics of literature. Television may be put down as the boob tube and a wasteland. But even as it is, television has widened the horizons of modern man and given him vistas of knowledge that would have been labeled miracles a half century ago. At the turn of a switch or a dial, almost any American may watch a man step on the moon or visit the Grand Canyon. He may enjoy from across a continent a sporting event or a Broadway play. He may watch Leonard Bernstein explain music to children in a way adults can understand. He may hear an artist, a philosopher, or a politician talk of his work and display an interesting lifestyle. An American may even go to school on television.

An Outhouse in Mid-Winter

Then there is the abundance, the variety and the quality of food available in this nation. In a world of famine and shortage, most Americans have fresh meat, fruits, and vegetables out of season. And all Americans eat better than kings did in previous centuries.

By illuminating the night, Edison gave the world—and particularly Americans—light and the gift of time.

Anyone who ever went to an outhouse in mid-winter in northern Maine, can be properly thankful for modern plumbing. This is the first generation to be clean—to take warm baths, to quickly and efficiently launder clothes and dishes, to control temperature despite the season, and to have pure water.

We have public parks, zoos, museums, libraries, swimming pools, athletic facilities, and shopping centers. All these are taken for granted, but all are new phenomena with origins only a century old.

A great many people are now alive because of medical advances in the last twenty years, and a majority of those over forty would not be alive if they had been born in another century. What about mobility? Before this day is out, anyone could be around the world. Most people may shop for the world's products within a few miles of their homes. Then there are professional sports, vacations, discretionary purchases, savings accounts, organized recreation, freedom to travel, freedom to change vocations, freedom of religion, time for leisure and relaxation—all part of the modern American's life, for the asking and the earning.

But even with as many material benefits, it is important to realize that the American system does not work on the basis of material things—whether it be in the electronic age with its modern miracles, or in the time of yesterday's abundant land. What a person owns is only useful for several generations at most, before it decays or is destroyed. The American system is not based on things but on innovation and ideas. The person who thinks about what he is doing, moves this economy—not the person who possesses lots of things.

It is the new idea which gives abundance. The first twenty-five years petroleum was refined, gasoline was thought to be worthless and was poured into the ground. Then someone got an idea—the internal combustion engine—and suddenly gasoline was a source of energy.

The transatlantic cable of copper weighed seventy-five thousand tons. Then a series of technological advances made telestar possible. Using less than a ton of materials, instantaneous television and greater communication were made possible. All the medical cures, new designs, new technologies, and new methods depend upon ideas.

Whale of an Oil Difference

W. Philip Gramm illustrates the process in the *Wall Street Journal,* November 30, 1973. In an attempt to put the current energy crisis in perspective, he describes the changeover from whale oil to petroleum. The major source of lighting throughout the first culture to the Civil War, in both America and Europe, was sperm oil. The supply of whales could not keep up with the demand, forcing up the price from 43¢ a gallon in 1823, to $2.55 a gallon in 1866. This encouraged the free enterprise system to look for and to exploit alternatives. With profit incentive and tremendous demand for the product, that energy crisis was met.

Unfortunately Gramm does not see the implication of his analysis. It was not the whale oil companies who met the need. They were so busy contemplating their own profits and product that they failed to see what was happening. Without exception they died rather than adjust or experiment. The process of capitalism and free enterprise, the economy of the first culture, was still in operation. As a result wild-catters and miners, still small entrepreneurs, moved in quickly. They had no large investments to protect, and stepped into the gap to provide energy for the exploding nation.

And ironically, it was their children who developed the modern tax system, which pays corporate farmers not to grow wheat and hogs, and gives depletion allowances to corporate giants— rather than tax advantages for research, environmental control and conservation. Now those industries, built in response to the first energy crisis, have so great a vested interest in present forms of energy and transportation that they appear unwilling or unable to provide new alternatives. With current governmental involvement and the enormous capital requirements in the field, a free market in energy is not possible as it was when the nation found that gasoline could supplant whale oil.

But if Americans concentrate on getting back the emphasis on appreciation and thanksgiving for all of life, and the challenge to improve life with new ideas, which were imbedded in the nation's first culture, they will create a fresh and revived perspective. They will inspire a climate in which problem solving can take place—including new forms of energy.

Communication and mobility are vital, if new ideas are to be effective. Although transportation was primitive, the first American culture was a time of great mobility. New towns and settlements were founded, the West was won, cities were built, and the first waves of immigration moved over the land. Most Americans are not aware that the mechanical age stopped that mobility. As industries were located on streams and close to supplies of raw material, they tended to attract workers to specific localities. Railroads brought all supplies to a common center. Then the system kept the working families in the same community for several generations.

Transportation facilities were rarely used for individual travel during the mechanical age. They were built and supported by commercial interests to transport merchandise from one location to another. Only the aristocratic few were able to travel. To be sure, the general populace romanticized the means of transportation. The locomotive, the steamboat, the horse and carriage, and finally the automobile, became vital symbols of American life. But it wasn't until after World War II that America recaptured the mobility of the frontier. During the first culture, man traveled only a few thousand miles in his lifetime. In this age he has reached the moon. But the psychological effect is the same—liberation, challenge, expanding horizons.

During the first culture, new paths were broken each day. As Indian trails became roads, citizens began to move. The settlements which marked the frontier give testimony to the mobility of the age. Slowly a network of post roads were constructed for mail delivery and commercial purposes. Individual and family travel followed the paths, not needing a developed road.

As late as 1789, there were only seventy-five post

offices in the republic. Magazines and newspapers had not yet been accepted by the postal service. Only a little over one thousand miles of post roads connected the major commercial towns.

One Letter Cost a Day's Pay

The mail stage, which could accommodate eleven passengers, made scheduled trips between towns with considerable difficulty. When everything went well, they were able to average eight miles an hour—but many delays could not be avoided. Poor weather and road conditions—rivers, mountains, lakes, stones, frequent relays of horse teams, broken equipment—all made travel an exhausting and exciting adventure. In a twenty-four hour span the fastest team, with perfect luck, could travel between 60 and 120 miles. The trip from Boston to Washington took a week. It took over a month to travel from Washington to New Orleans. Travelers had to make unscheduled stops in many villages. Layovers of a week or more were not unusual, if the stage had been damaged. Travel by public or private means involved frequent stops at private homes.

But with mail service unreliable and expensive—one letter cost eight cents or a day's pay to go thirty miles, and more than twice as much to go 150 miles—and with no other means of communication available, many villagers were encouraged to travel.

It is incredible, but as the means of transportation increased, people became more provincial. Throughout the 18th century, when conditions were generally primitive, a great number of Americans—as much as 5% of the population—traveled to Europe. Many more took trips along the coastline. Travel documents show the extent and the frequency of their journeys. Primary motivation for travel in that time, was the pursuit of cultural improvement. The Grand Tour became part of an American education. In the mechanical age the vast majority of Americans were concentrated in industrial centers without time or opportunity to travel anywhere except to and from work. At the same time, those who remained on the farm were isolated by both poverty and provincialism. A far smaller percentage of Americans were able to travel. And those who did usually had business or political reasons for doing so.

Communication practices produced much the same result. When a messenger traveled from town to town with important news, that news entered into general circulation. When mail service was improved and made regular, the most important information was taken out of the public trust.

Today the Inn has Changed

During the first culture, travelers were also constantly thrown together in the coach, in the inn at meals, and even in the bedroom, where it was common for twelve unrelated guests to share the same sleeping quarters. The tavern was also the only place of entertainment for both travelers and villagers, drawing them together naturally.

In the early days of the 18th century, every town had several taverns or inns. They gave colonial villages vital contacts with the outside world. No place was so remote that it did not have its share of travelers bringing news and cultural inspiration from all parts of the world, transforming the intellectual and artistic life of the village. All creative people who traveled had to stop in many small villages, and the kind of accommodations available to them assured personal involvement with village residents. With improvements in transportation, however, and travelers able to make the trip from one major population center to another in a day, only urban centers could maintain inns and hotels.

Today, the inn itself has changed. The hotels of the

mechanical age were built for privacy. Every step was taken to assure that guests would not "disturb" one another. Such isolation was especially the lot of prominent leaders in every field. Thus, the very people who held court in the taverns of the first culture were out of general circulation in the mechanical age. Today, in the electronic age, they are the guests on the talk shows.

With the advent of the mechanical age came the American system of conventions, and business meetings developed as a regular part of hotel life. Individuals were together for entertainment and for light chatter, but business and cultural topics were always presented in formal sessions, usually without the embarrassment of discussion. This procedure, begun by the powerful business barons of the mechanical age, assured that eventually a small group of professional managers would rise to power. As enterprises became enormous in size, with thousands of stockholders, the process of ownership had to be formalized. The stockholder was removed from all centers of real information and power.

A Family Centered Lifestyle

The great business of America throughout the period of the first culture was, of course, agriculture. In 1770, eighty percent of Americans were farmers, men making their living from the land. In the total population of over two million, only 18% were artisans, the remaining 2% gentlemen. But even those individuals who followed a craft or a profession, also worked a self-sufficient farm. By the nineteenth century, the entire population in cities of over 5,000 inhabitants, was only 16% of the whole population. And in those days before extensive immigration, even city residents were likely to have been reared on the farm.

This made inevitable the development of a family-centered lifestyle. A perfect form in which to work out the Biblical injunction "Be fruitful and multiply," the family became also the spiritual, cultural, political and economic center of colonial life. Every person could better find identity, the crucial experiences of love, emotional and spiritual growth, and psychological and physical security, within a small, intimate group. Here the person was needed, and could find fulfillment for personal needs. In the first culture, the family group was the agent for this dynamic growth.

The freedom of the great empty spaces encircled the farmer from the beginning. Each family farm had open lands for pasture, cultivated gardens, and some forest. The farmer welcomed the freshness of his new life. But, paradoxically, the natural wonder of the country and its spaciousness is not recorded to any great extent in studies of the American cultural heritage.

Nature Seen As Enemy

Farming in America, especially along the rocky eastern coastline, never involved much nature worship. As often as not, nature was seen as the enemy. Farming was hard work. It was rarely romanticized, and then usually by nonfarmers. For the farmer, nature was hardly benign. He had to deal with drought and windstorm, flash floods and driving hailstorms. The snows of winter were a constant challenge.

On the farm, the work each member of the family performed was vital. Children helped with the planting, weeding and harvesting. They gathered firewood, looked after the chickens, and cared for the younger animals. Wives and older daughters not only cared for the kitchen and the house, they worked vegetable and flower gardens. They made their own clothes, candles, medicines, and baskets. The father and older boys did the major share of construction. They made tools, utensils and furniture. They cleared land, and cared for the slaughter and dressing of the larger animals. All members of the family worked together on the major seasonal tasks.

However—even though the family worked hard— the work pace was set according to the natural rhythms of the human body. Adjustments were also made for personal desires and abilities. A man worked at his own pace. His wife was the only "efficiency expert" with whom he had to contend. A particularly beautiful day might find him fishing, or taking an excursion. The family learned to make games of much hard work. Since the seasons set the clock, there was also little sense of being in a hurry. A man had time to meditate, to read, to visit the tavern, and had time for conversation and a social life. There was great variety and challenge in the work.

During the winter, great buckets were made from the trunks of large trees. The farmer cut his staves and was his own cooper in the making of barrels. Tools and utensils were hand-made and mended, furniture and buildings were constructed and repaired, and produce was brought to market. Each spring brought the sugaring season. The land was planted, and the stock pastured. With the summer came fishing, hunting and gardening. In October the grain threshing, harvesting and haying, varied the workload and the pattern of the day's labor. Before snow came, hogs were slaughtered and cooked, and the woodpile carefully stacked. And the family would make excursions in all seasons—to the grist mill, the saw mill, the potter, the tavern, and especially, to church.

The Farmer's Life Had Meaning

Is it only sentimental to suggest that the life of the village offered a kind of reality that motivated the farmer's idealism? He was a complete man with time to cultivate his body, mind and soul. His life was hard, but the farmer had few problems with either self-identity or self-image. He took pride in his work, and in his accomplishments. His sex life, while unchronicled, was remarkably productive. The small evidence we have indicates it was an activity of splendid joy as well. His life had meaning. His goals were secure. His work had purpose, and he was needed. The family shared these advantages.

Scientific methods of farming—rotation of crops, purebred stock, time saving machinery, and conservation of natural resources—were not quickly accepted in America. The natural abundance gave little stimulus to change. Ambition was for a good life, not the ultimate in accumulation and consumption. A farmer who had enough to provide the essentials for his family felt rewarded for his life work.

From Industrial to Service Economy

Just before the Civil War, only 4% of the nation's population was involved in manufacturing of any kind. Then in less than a hundred years, the transformation from agriculture to industry was almost complete. Now the electronic age has initiated another sweeping change—from an industrial to a service economy. There are several obvious parallels between work experience in agriculture and in service: considerable individual control of time and work methods; more personal and multi-dimensional involvement with other people; success more directly based on individual performance; substantial release from the psychological pressures of working in fields of constant technological change; and, unorganized and unprotected by unions, both types of workers are subject to failure as a result of circumstance wholly beyond individual control—the weather or a major change in consumer taste.

And, of course, electronic media make the same

family-centered form of life relevant today in any pursuit of happiness. A complex, pluralistic society, thrown out of balance by the enormous power of huge bureaucratic institutions, is more dependent than ever upon a family-centered lifestyle. Personal habits developed by this way of living in our first culture provided a foundation for the developing economy. Family life emphasized personal cleanliness, diligence, thrift, self-reliance, independence, pride, and for many—integrity, faith and joy. It can do the same thing for the people living in this electronic age.

Personal Dependence Upon Integrity and Ethics

Basic hangups of the American character must also be confronted if the nation's economy is to be made right. The real shortage facing the American economy is not of material resources. It is of ethical resources. And fortunately, ethical resources are renewable, and may be reclaimed. A basic lesson of the first culture involved such renewal and reclamation. Criminals, debtors, the poor, the infirm, the unwanted, the unloved, came to these shores. Many were able to develop character in the new world, because here they were free to change, to receive the fruits of their labor, to feel needed and wanted by those about them. Freedom for them was not an abstraction. It was a reality.

They found here land and resources beyond dreams. And if they didn't like life on the coast, if they didn't feel accepted, they just moved on to the West. With every difficult experience, they were free to move. Squatters rights was more than a term of legal history. Some realized the moral crisis and established roots. Others had to move all the way to the west coast before they realized the emptiness was inside. But once the individual was free to be himself, free inside, he was able to reshape his character. From his Bible he learned that freedom was something that

39

had to be claimed. The Puritan believed that freedom came only from Jesus Christ. Only when a person found the meaning of life was he free; free to be the self the creator intended him to be. This freedom resulted in the strong independence and personal integrity so common among early Americans. And upon this spiritual resource the economic foundations of a nation were built.

Old Fashioned Virtues

Integrity and personal morality may seem like old-fashioned virtues. However, no capitalistic system of economics can exist without them. Corruption in government and in the marketplace, and dishonesty on the job and in advertising, can bring any economy down. So can theft of material goods or corrupt business practice, injustice in the society and in the writing of law, and malignant selfishness in private and corporate life.

The basic system of craftsmanship and personal responsibility which originally brought vitality to this nation, cannot survive without integrity and ethical responsibility. Andre Malraux has written the epitaph of any civilization that is indifferent to spiritual values: "I believe that the civilization of the machine is the first civilization which has no supreme value for the majority of men ... It remains to be seen whether a civilization can exist only as a civilization of questioning or of the moment, and whether it can base its values for long on something other than a religion."

Only when pre-Revolutionary America is compared to the mechanical age, can we see that it is not capitalism which has caused our current difficulties. It is aberrations in that system, brought about by the washing away of its foundations. Capitalism has worked only when backed by a strong religious heritage. This provided commonly accepted goals and

values, a rigorous ethic to furnish standards of jus-
justice and equality in the community, and integrity
and responsibility in private life. In the mechanical
age this foundation was lost. Qualitative goals of
religion were replaced by quantitative goals of production.

Values were not sectarian in the first culture. One
genius of the American experience was the pervasiveness of spiritual force in the new land. Most activities
were personalized, humanized and made holy, not by
religious fiat, but by a commonly experienced benevolence. Although few were active in the church,
nearly all accepted the same, non-materialistic definition of the good life. The mechanical age corrupted
the natural, built-in ethical advantages of capitalism.

Legislation to Rig the Market

The capitalistic system valued the good work of
the craftsman, motivated hard and honest labor, rewarded thrift and innovation, supported freedom and
liberty as a lifestyle, and was tuned to the desires and
needs of the general public. It was suddenly overwhelmed by speculators, government interference and
criminal activity. Speculators who defraud the public,
take no risk themselves, provide no service or innovation, and are not part of the capitalist system. Massive
and corrupt distribution of governmental resources is
also equally foreign to effective capitalism, as are the
granting of exclusive privileges and the use of legislation to rig the market or provide advantage to the
powerful.

Capitalism, especially as seen in the villages of the
first culture, accommodated change successfully only
when a base of integrity and ethical standards was
maintained. Success in business has always come
when leaders were creative enough to scrap not only
worn out buildings and systems, but also old ideas,
old customs, old formulas, and old objectives. The

only thing that cannot be scrapped is ethical values. The greatest thing about capitalism has been its ability to adapt and change according to principles of supply and demand. As the mechanical age comes to an end, business has lost the one dynamic factor that gave it power—its ability to value and make change.

The mechanical age begins roughly around 1800. It runs through to 1960 when the electronic age begins. This age actually developed from discoveries, breakthroughs, and inventions which began in the 1920's and 1930's. While it is perfectly obvious there is considerable fudging and overlapping in any definition of any so-called age—for the purpose of simplification, this book will use 1820 to 1960 as the mechanical age, and beyond that the electronic age.

The mechanical age brought Social Darwinism to this nation, a doctrine that allowed only for the survival of the fittest. This seemed possible in a simplistic society, which allowed the demands of productivity to define the only possible standard of success. But in this electronic age which is upon us, there is incredible complexity and utter dependence upon sophisticated technical information, too intricate for any single individual or organization to assimilate. A doctrine of survival of the fittest is meaningless. The successful entrepreneur of the mechanical age—aggressive, individualistic, competitive, intuitive, willing to gamble, and able to risk all—is a nostalgic memory in the real world. The modern technostructure demands not aggression, but sensitivity. It needs not individualism, but group action; not competition, but cooperation; not intuition, but corporate planning; not waste, but conservation. Most important of all, it needs not smoothness, but integrity.

Ironically, there are no values, if all values are for sale. Men and women are deeply discontented today in both blue and white collar jobs, which serve only materialistic goals. The passing of the mechanical age, and the moving in of the electronic age is evidenced in the decline of labor unions, and the growth of an educated class which feels itself superior to both advertising claims and menial vocations. On the crest of its wave is the inability of the white collar worker to retire, the empty satisfaction of success in the business world, the inability of government to stabilize and enhance the quality of life.

The Demon of Specialized Slaves

The citizen of the electronic age, aware of the power of the atom and tiny transistors, has psychologically rejected bigness as the only criteria of evaluation. Aesthetic, ethical and qualitative considerations are pushing aside factors which can be easily quantified. The best of America's young suddenly realized that society had created the demon of the specialized slave, who had no time to find happiness and quality in life. In management or in science, in technology or in education, in business or in industry, the specialized slave sought increased production in a never ending cycle. Even proximate success was always in the future, in the chance of exceeding the performance of the year before. The present, where all of life is lived, was always overwhelmed by the specialized task. Few could give any attention to the whole fabric of life. Success was always partial and incomplete, inevitably frustrating and self-defeating.

At the same time, the evidence of material success, once self-sufficient, was no longer psychologically satisfying. Military power was suddenly ineffective as a method to realize national goals, and war itself was no longer respected as a means of change by intelligent people. Successful production and ever increasing consumption had, in fact, raped the land of its abundance. It had mortgaged the future of the environment for a few moments of present indulgence. The public relations and advertising system which sustained production, eventually eroded both integrity and values. As everything was claimed, nothing seemed believable.

Americans, that are now over forty, did not watch a single hour of television before they were graduated from high school. The average graduate of today has already spent 23,000 hours watching the tube. His cynicism has been carefully cultivated. Literally he has had to assimilate thousands of exaggerated claims, heard political promises and double-talk, and watched the development of the "star system" of success in all areas of public life (entertainment, sports, politics, business, and even the arts). He has seen that this type of success often has little to do with talent, and rarely rewards either integrity or an altruistic system or values.

What is evident in this is that the values of the mechanical age were possible only as long as the majority had limited horizons. The graphic and instantaneous protrayal of injustice, inequity, and inhumanity transformed both the perception and the opinion of a generation. While fathers were limited as specialists, sons and daughters took time to become generalists—interested in all areas of life and in all sections of the world. Thousands of the most able of the nation's young could no longer be forced to fit an antiquated educational system and vocational market.

In 1900, the average American traveled 30,000 miles in a lifetime. By 1970, the average had become a million miles. Many businessmen have traveled well over three million miles and an astronaut covered that distance in orbit in less than a week. For the first time, a significant number of people are able to have the same humanizing contacts and cultural information on a world scale, that was previously available only in a village society.

Vested Interests Take Over

And, for the first time in the current economic

crisis, Americans no longer display their innate, naive optimism. The leadership seems to doubt the system will work. Americans have not often been so discouraged. Many innovations and inventions were first discovered in Europe, but the possibilities were unrealized because too many there had a stake in the old way of doing things, to embrace and try anything new. Americans, on the other hand, were rarely held back by vested interests, or by the pressures of habit. They were always ready to experiment and to attempt innovation. Europe fell behind, as privilege and power corrupted its capitalistic system. Inevitably this same process came to America with the mechanical age. Vested interests of all types corrupted the capitalistic system, and caused the injustices and inequities for which it is justly criticized. Simply because all the original goals of Americans have been realized, we are more restive. There is confusion in abundance, because we have not articulated new goals that can be shared by all.

But this writer is convinced that the combination of the four spiritual strengths of early America—the Puritan work ethic, the conviction that natural resources are providentially provided, a family-centered lifestyle, and a necessary foundation of integrity and ethical standards—can bring vitality to our economy and to our lives. Only spiritual strength can make this once abundant land abundant again. Motivation in the economy must always be spiritual, for every person needs to be needed, the individual has to have some worthwhile accomplishments, needs to love and be loved, to share a mandate for justice, and to seek a meaning in life.

In the electronic age no worker manufactures a finished product. For this reason all members of society become increasingly dependent upon society as a whole. All relationships tend to become more complex and impersonal, at just the time when individuals demand more security and a sense of personal worth. It is an incredibly difficult challenge to structure spiritual values within such a complex economy and society. But without facing that hard challenge, no justice, no liberty, and no general pursuit of happiness is possible. Thanks to modern technology, the demand for more humanized work can be met if the foundations of capitalism are reclaimed. The strong religious heritage of the first culture provided goals and values which are still viable, when combined with standards of justice and equality in public life.

Harbingers of Reclamation of First Culture

Already there are harbingers of reclaiming the essentials of the first culture in major sections of the business community:

—Businesses are decentralizing, giving more autonomy to geographically separate operations, and recognizing that decisions are best made by those closest to the problem.

—Business is broadening the scope of its responsibility to include the public sector and the general quality of life.

—Business is giving, for the first time, substantial financial support to both educational and artistic institutions, and giving commissions to individual artists.

—Generalists are more likely to attain top management positions. Broadly trained and aware of America's cultural heritage, they know where to get technical information, and how to use it. No longer are basic decisions made by the narrow specialist or, even by an individual businessman.

—Japan and Germany have proven that an economy can be healthy and growing without dependence on the armaments industry.

—Ralph Nader's consumerism has demanded the

old integrity in the marketplace and social responsibility at the highest levels of industry.

—Business is recognizing the priorities and importance of the public sector of the economy: housing, health care, mass transportation, education, sanitation, conservation, and crime prevention.

—In response to the demand for generalists, educational emphasis in business schools and universities is radically changing. Suddenly no specialty can be intellectually isolated from the whole range of science and humanities. Business schools, which throughout the mechanical age taught only practical and specialized courses, now provide sophisticated coverage of social psychology, electronic systems, data processing, government and politics, ethics, aesthetics and design, and even courses in general culture and history.

But these are only beginnings. The business community has a long way to go to recapture the goals and values which grew naturally in the abundant land. Yet, there is a new appreciation of the value of the capitalistic system, unfettered by the aberration of government interference and corruption. A realization is emerging that this system was able to handle the problems of the first culture because it was based on a foundation of ethics and humanity. With a similar foundation, it may well provide the key to the future.

Is the 2 Nation's Lifestyle Collapsing?

Uncertainty in Go-Getter Morality

Without thinking much about it, the great majority of Americans have accepted a success ethic. In every area of human activity, winning is the defined good, valued more for the achievement, than for any substantive result. Parents commonly pressure their young to succeed in school, in dating, in popularity, in sports, and in the economy. Goals which could not be quantified, have been too abstract to receive attention. Since there is no possibility of ultimate success, no achievement is permanently satisfying. Success itself is always pushed into the future, a goal never to be realized. This go-getter morality has created general uncertainty, because that which is good is always fluctuating somewhere in the future. With no recognized criteria of truth, the success ethic describes a lifestyle, but provides no standard. Americans pursue life, liberty, and happiness without reference to Biblical ethics. Thus far it is not working. The accomplishments of material success, financial success, power success, and prestige success, have brought increased expectations—but no self-realization.

The success disease which has infected the country has also infected most individual Americans. And by its own standards, it has not been successful either for the nation or for individuals. Almost all the great problems of our time are a direct result of the success ethic. Those who worry about the environment and pollution, realize that the doctrines of conspicuous consumption, of obsolescence, of unlimited production and use of raw materials, and of a single standard of profitability, are creatures of the success ethic. Those interested in the poor, the oppressed, the downtrodden, realize you cannot have a success ethic without, by implication, labeling all those who are not powerful or materially affluent, as failures. A majority of Americans have to live their lives, warped by a self-image shaped by those who deal in the success ethic. The slums of our cities, the crime in our streets, the impersonalism of our society—where people are identified by number and even come to think of themselves as numbers—and the blind nationalism which leads to war, all stem from the success ethic. That which breeds selfishness and pride in personal life, rewards arrogance and superficiality in public life.

Infiltrated by Success Ethic

Most tragic of all, people labeled successful, affluent and powerful, find their lives in shambles. When they reach their goal, they find it is not a goal at all. Their goods and possessions have eaten them up. Family life has been broken apart more often by the images of success, than by any other single cause. All areas of life, from sex to parenthood, have been infiltrated by the success ethic. Women have been caught both ways—by definition unable to succeed by the standards set by men, and yet condemned to the

50

empty images of success. All minority groups have been cemented into the same dilemma.

Today there is not one prodigal son, but hundreds of thousands. There are parents who seem not to care, and do not know how to forgive. There are so many incidents of corruption that success itself can no longer be defined.

It is time for Americans to go back to their ethical roots to a lifestyle not yet infected by the disease stemming from the mechanical age. Two hundred years ago Americans didn't have perfection. The colonial fathers faced many of the difficulties experienced today. In addition, they faced terrors resulting from national weakness, natural catastrophe, and health hazards.

In many ways the childhood of a nation is like that of an individual—a time to come to terms with life. Through action and reaction, that which is important becomes increasingly apparent. The structure of a family allows individual growth in the same way as does the structure of government. When accomplished successfully, just enough restraint leads to a basic security. Just enough freedom leads to spontaneous creativity.

Although governed from abroad throughout most of the period of the first culture, Americans had surprising autonomy because of the great distance to the motherland, the poor means of transportation and communication, and the natural independence of those adventurous enough to be explorers and pioneers. The politics of America from the first, was a politics of abundance, interested in the rapid growth of wealth, rather than in dividing it with justice and equality. From the beginning the frontier was a force for nationalism and for democracy. The threat of the French and the Indians consolidated the colonies when they wished to be apart. That menace made mandatory common forts and a national militia. The increasingly mobile population and the empty space worked together to destroy provincialism. The frontier formed a melting pot for a diversified mixture of Europeans.

Puritans believed that the King, when he talked about his divine right to rule, claimed a prerogative to which only God was entitled. They taught that the government was for the people's welfare, not the people for the government's welfare. They believed with John Locke that "Man is an appropriating animal, commanded by God to subdue the earth." Nature's wealth was there for all to claim. It was this abundance that defined the role of government in the first culture. Land was surveyed, given exact boundaries, and its ownership determined. It then had to be defended from Indians, Europeans and unruly fellow citizens. Most important, the government established the rules which made the land available and determined its value. Political policy determined accessibility, through roads, turnpikes, canals, and eventually the railroad. It determined security by defining and protecting integrity of ownership. And it fixed responsibility or the extent of taxation, public service, road building, common pastureland, and militia duty.

The Safety Valve of the West

Throughout the first culture, the safety valve of the West minimized the effect of inequality and injustice. While only those with property could vote, and only those with greater wealth could hold public office, as long as a person was free to go West and seek his own stake of abundance, injustice was a personal experience rather than a national condition. However, when the frontier was gone, this heritage of individualism and self-reliance began to work against justice. The powerful were able to make sacred a definition of freedom, which protected property while ignoring human rights. The poor man was considered a failure. Persons receiving welfare were

52

required to wear a badge. A large red "P" for pauper was required in New Jersey. Before the twentieth century, the national government took no responsibility for human welfare, excepting for veterans' programs. In fact, the Social Security Act of 1935 was the first permanent welfare program for the general population, participated in by the Federal government.

Ethical considerations are always vital for those who live in a democracy. Unless ethical standards are commonly accepted and adhered to, democracy becomes an exercise in corruption and power. (While it is the best method to establish justice with the foundation of a shared ethic, democracy is at the same time most easily corrupted when the ethical foundation erodes.) Because the Constitution had established a balance of power between the executive, the legislature and the judiciary, people could appeal all decisions to the courts. In such a system of government, there was always hope for the oppressed and protection for the minority. The very first Supreme Court decision, handed down on August 11, 1792, was made with two justices dissenting. Chief Justice Hughes defined a dissent as "an appeal to the broadening spirit of the law, to the intelligence of a future day."

When Jefferson, during his Presidency, liberalized the nationalization and immigration laws, purchased the Louisiana Territory, and gave public attention to education, he gave permanence to the democratic tradition. The first move assured a constant infusion of diverse cultural traditions into the American experience, and gave that infusion support within the political system. The second opened up the entire country, assuring the perpetuation of the first culture for another fifty years, and the mobility of society. The last laid the groundwork for universal suffrage.

The first culture had a broad democratic foundation The democratic principles within the church policy of Congregationalism, made it inevitable that the Puritans would be a liberating force despite themselves. Their faith gave them a source of authority, which enabled them to defy their political peers around the world. The King could be attacked, first of all, because he interfered with the working of the covenant. As Cromwell's career abundantly demonstrated, the Royal power never was considered by Puritans.

Their faith was equally influential in establishing the unique worth and dignity of every individual. This worth, a gift of God, which had little to do with personal capacity or accomplishment, made a political doctrine of equality inevitable.

Democracy in Puritan Tradition

Puritan faith also provided, before it was corrupted, a spirit of humility and toleration which allowed the construction of a pluralistic society. Although much bigotry and prejudice is found in American history, such a response is never an authentic outgrowth of Puritanism. Only a few pastors, soon left behind by their parishoners, held out for an exclusive, theocratic state. All the crucial teachings of Christianity allow openness in a pluralistic society. The Witchcraft trials and early persecutions, while reprehensible, were American exaggerations of what was then a worldwide phenomena. Considering the volatile history of the United States, it is amazing how little religious persecution there has been.

It was the faith of the Puritans that inspired Americans to challenge tyranny, whether in church or state. Democratic systems have arisen primarily in lands influenced by Puritan traditions, because Puritans saw so clearly that when God alone is sovereign, all other powers are subject to restraint. Unrestricted power can be granted to no one. With this sense of responsibility to God alone, Puritans provided the spiritual foundation for a democratic society. This was the case, even though many Puritans were so interested in establishing a society which reflected God from top to bottom, that they did not see this implication of their faith.

Those who gathered to write the Constitution were not as likely to embrace democratic principles. They spoke essentially for the privileged classes, far more influenced by plantation life than by the village culture. Edmund Randolph told the Constitutional Convention that "the evils from which the country suffered originated in the turbulence and follies of democracy, and that the great danger lay in the democratic parts of our constitutions." Eldridge Gerry spoke of democracy as "the worst of all political evils." Roger Sherman hoped that "the people have as little to do" with governing as possible. William Livingston claimed that "the people have ever been and ever will be unfit to exercise power in their own hands." George Washington, who presided, urged the delegates not to approve any document simply "in order to please the people." Hamilton charged that the "turbulent and changing" masses "seldom judge or determine right," and suggested that a permanent governmental body "check the imprudence of democracy." One wealthy young planter, Charles Pinckney, moved that no one be allowed to run for President who was not worth at least one hundred thousand dollars. These comments are not out of context, but quite representative of the political leadership of the convention.

It is estimated that over 90% of those convicted for crimes in the years 1800-1830, were convicted for offenses against property. In 1829 the Prison Discipline Society reported that 75,000 people were imprisoned for debt in the United States, and that more than half owed less than $20.

Jefferson's DECLARATION OF INDEPENDENCE was based on the philosophy of Locke, not on the theology of the Puritans. He spoke of the "natural" and "inalienable" rights of man, rather than of those derived from any covenant. Essentially equalitarian, it showed the influence of French thought. By itself, the Declaration would have left a modest base for a working democracy, since its two great assertions—liberty and equality—are essentially in conflict with one another, except when they are carefully structured by justice, and understood in reference to God's creation and covenant. Individuals are not by nature equal in physical strength, mental capacity, or in force of personality. If left with full liberty to compete with one another, without limitations of justice, they soon would be unequal in power, wealth, prestige and leisure. Without some qualification, liberty and equality are in irreconcilable conflict in a complex civilization.

Means to Extend Liberty and Equality

All men are equal only in the light of God's creation. They are unequal in every other discernable way.

Whenever a democracy allows complete freedom, it will soon produce an aristocracy which will have the power to rule—a military-industrial-university complex. This was in fact the social situation at the time of the Constitutional Convention. Whenever a democracy allows unrestricted equalitarianism, it drifts toward a totalitarianism supported by a majority of the people. This problem, in itself, gave the political leverage necessary to reconcile the Declaration and the Constitution, and to convince the fathers that an element of democracy was essential for republican government. The eighteenth century philosophy, which formed the Declaration, was almost totally inappropriate for the mechanical age to which it was applied. The complexities of modern civilization demanded a state, which was constantly attempting to balance liberty and equality. Flexibility and changeability were the needed qualities for an effective government. The Constitution, instead of the brilliantly phrased Declaration, became the fundamental document of American democracy, for it could be changed, modified, and formally interpreted.

When Washington was inaugurated as President, the system of government in the United States could hardly have been called "democracy." Only one in seven free, adult males could vote. Property and education were considerations which excluded the vast majority from franchise. Women would not be free to vote for a century and a half. Most black Americans had to wait for almost two centuries. Yet, the Constitution provided the means for extending both liberty and equality.

The unique feature of the developing democracy was not the rule of the majority. As early as 1791, John Quincy Adams answered Thomas Paine's *Rights of Man,* which claimed as inviolate doctrine, that the will of the majority must always prevail. Adams persuasively argued that "the violation of the immutable laws of justice was not within the rights of the majority." The unique feature of the developing democracy was rather the protection of the rights of the various minorities. This feature, particularly vital for cultural growth, was neglected during the mechanical age.

Democracy, then, can never be an end, a perfect goal, for government. It is, rather, a means to an end.

Jefferson's prophesy that democracy could work only as long as differences in wealth and power are kept within reasonable limits, has proved historically correct. There must be a certain minimum of equality.

Adams was equally correct in his prophesy that democracy would survive only as long as man had freedom to use the fruits of his talent and labor. There must be a certain minimum of liberty.

The great size and bureaucratic power of government in the nation today have compromised the democratic system. Change is much harder to effect, because the process of entrenchment and vested interest is almost absolute, especially within the governmental structure itself. The federal government has become the leading factor in the economy. From 20 to 25% of all economic activity is now accounted for by the various levels of government. In 1929, federal, state and local governments together accounted for less than 8% of the nation's economic activity. The current percentage substantially exceeds that for several socialist states—India, Sweden and Norway—and is only slightly below that of Great Britain and the communist state of Poland.

In addition, the federal government has invaded every area of life: regulating, taxing, licensing, fixing prices and wages, setting acreage and marketing quotas, manipulating the supply of food, money and services, and establishing interest rates. The Keynesian theory that the state should directly intervene in every crisis is now universal policy. This advance in the power of government was made both possible and inevitable by the forces of the mechanical age. Urban concentration, industrial development, population explosion, national marketing, and the inability of the states to develop and supervise transportation, control big business corporations, and the exploitation of natural resources, all made federal power necessary.

As long as the ethical foundation sustained the lives of the great majority, the democratic system worked. Government, business, home life and industry all depended upon the thrifty, honest, industrious, fair, temperate, and faithful individual. Early Americans, many of whom did not believe in orthodox Christianity, nevertheless shared a common, agreed upon ethic. Even those who were not Christians had absorbed the Christian ethic and their values were shaped by its heritage. Thomas Jefferson, a Deist, lifted up the ethics of Christ. Benjamin Franklin, a liberal philosopher, lifted up the ethics of Christ. George Washington, a Christian, lifted up the ethics of Christ. Even Thomas Paine, an Atheist, despite himself, lifted up the ethics of Christ. Alexander Hamilton, a pragmatist, lifted up the ethics of Christ. The whole society was built upon and absorbed, often unknowingly, the ethics of Christ. This is the leading difference between that time and the present. If we are to reclaim a democratic society in its entirety, the same ethical foundation, whatever it is to be called, will be necessary.

In the Old Testament, there is no individualistic ethic at all. In contrast, the success ethic is totally individualist and selfish, lifting up precisely those qualities which Christ condemned, pride and greed. The Old Testament defined ethics in such a way, that no one could be a success unless all were successful. In covenant, human activity had to conform to the will of God. Activity is guided, not by convention, but by God's command. Since God created all mankind, He commands that we love one another, and be humble in our relationships with one another. Christian ethics is essentially one's response to God as creator of all. His commands, "Be not anxious for your life" and "Love thy neighbor as thyself," are essential in the quest for happiness. The Puritans served Him as an act of thanksgiving for the gifts of creation. Appreciation for this rare gift of life is the basis for all ethics. Early Americans knew the lesson that there was no separation between the spiritual and the secular. They were too wrapped up in life, to separate their faith from it. They had learned the Biblical lesson that a Christian had to be involved in the sinful world, despite dangers of contamination.

A concern for every individual, irrespective of past conduct or present ability, is the first mark of a Christian. Understanding that all men are sinners, the Christian is under the explicit command of not judging another human being. Concern for all people, reflecting the compassion of a God who cares desperately, gave the first culture its ideals. Of course early Americans failed to live up to those ideals, but those ideals were the self-conscious goals of that society. Although offering no panacea, the shared goals did develop the individual habits and corporate responsibility necessary for the American experiment. Until corrupted by the values and ethics of the mechanical age, Americans were in the process of developing a lifestyle worthy of the first governmental system which attempted "freedom and justice for all."

The insulated, emotionless diety, a creature of the industrial revolution, is the opposite of the Christian God. In every parable Jesus told, there is a picture of a God who cares. These stories of compassion allow people to see others as human beings. Male and female, black and white, Muslim and Jew, German and French, rich and poor, all are equally precious to God. Each individual name and each hair on every head, are known by God. Only love is intrinsically good. Love, not success, brings happiness.

Americans of revolutionary times had a great advantage. Their life was still the life of the village, and they had personal relationships with everyone around them. So often today's Americans are isolated and impersonal, made to appear more selfish than they really are by computers and the mechanisms of society. Empathy and sympathy are often set aside by the impersonalism of modern life. At some point, Americans came to accept in the name of their government, ethical actions which they would never accept in their own lives.

A feeling of empathy for the least powerful, and of humility concerning one's own virtues, is a beginning. The time may soon be coming when all will have to live in a "steady state" or "spaceman" economy, where reserves of raw materials and foodstuffs are exhausted, and life is limited to that which can be renewed year by year. Americans lived in a similar circumstance until well after the revolution, and developed ethical standards and individual habits to meet the needs of such a world. Then came the "success ethic," where even the successful are condemned by their own success. Giants of industry find themselves empty and completely unsatisfied; the powerful find that they cannot communicate with their own children; the wealthy find that no amount of possessions are satisfying; and the most prestigious find that they cannot respect themselves. How many millions have worked for thirty years toward a goal and reached it, only to find nothing worthwhile?

Grace in the Humble

Any new lifestyle must be based on humility, the foundation of New Testament ethics. The quality of humility is stressed more than any other in the Gospel. In the teaching of Jesus, it is the proud who will be brought low, and the humble who will be exhalted. The way into the kingdom of God is the path of a child's humility. God gives grace to the humble. Christ himself is the suffering servant, the one who gives up glory to live as a servant. The pattern of New Testament humility is found on the cross. The servant is needed and loved. Happiness comes in being needed and loved.

In the world of the success ethic, little premium is accorded humility. The humble rarely have sufficient competitive spirit. They are often misfits in terms of the success lifestyle. Yet it is the American experience, both in history and in contemporary life, that

61

those who reach a state of happiness, who have integrity, and love justice, are, without exception, the possessors of humility.

The success ethic is never helpful at the extremities of life. It has no answer for the loss of a son or a husband, for critical illness, for self-realization, for self-respect, or for happiness. Even by the pragmatic standards of the success ethic itself, the only lifestyle that consistently works is that founded on the Biblical Word as expressed in Micah 6:8: "O man, what is good; and what does the Lord require of you but to do justice, and to love kindness, and to walk humbly with your God."

Is **3** *AmericanCulture Crumbling?*

> *"We want a national literature with our mountains and rivers . . . We want a national epic that shall correspond to the size of the country . . . We want a national drama in which scope shall be given to our gigantic ideas and to the unparalleled activity of our people."*
>
> Henry Wadsworth Longfellow, 1849.

A Culture Attracted to the Wild

During the seventeenth and eighteenth centuries, the abundant land shaped American culture in all its forms.

The art of the nation's first culture was unable to ignore the land and therefore investigated its mystery, power, challenge, and beauty. It was inspired by a sense of the primitive, and pervaded by a persistent attempt to preserve basic values. The young nation's whole culture was attracted to the wild, free landscape of the new world. Summarizing this heritage, Thoreau wrote: "In wilderness is the preservation of the World . . . From the forest and wilderness come the tonics and barks which move mankind. . .".

Developing legends had a primitive innocence. Paul Bunyan could cover an entire state with a single stride. Davy Crockett could "walk like an ox, run like a fox, swim like an eel, yell like an Indian, fight like a devil, sprout like an earthquake, and make love like a bull." Everything was exaggerated, because the land was so great, so fresh, so rich. Yet its natural

63

environment was older than Europe itself. Here was creation, the mysterious beginnings of the human race, a true foundation for empire and destiny. In the wilderness, the darkness could be sensed as a terrible power, which would interrupt the errand of innocents. The creative energy of Americans was given to the work of discovery, survival, settlement, theology and government, and it was these themes which motivated its culture in its first two centuries. Under pressure of events, Americans were willing to dispense with all art for art's sake.

The Puritan as Artist

In spite of hardship, the citizen of that first culture had several advantages over the contemporary American. For one thing, with the average life-span of thirty-five years, it was easy to dramatize the importance of time. And Puritanism, while it did seriously restrict the actor or thespian, was a beneficial force in all other areas of the arts. Its doctrine on work resulted in a participatory culture in which everyone did for himself, in the arts as in other areas of life. Its glorification of creation gave early Americans a new appreciation for nature and natural wonders. Ironically, its very prohibition of idolatry opened up the whole world to the artist. The same impetus which banned sacred themes, the sole subject matter permitted for centuries, presented the artist with the whole secular world. Also, the art of early America was an amateur art. There was no money to support professionals, and it was free of the control of patrons or customers. Suddenly the creative could work in any style they wished, free to receive stimulus from any secular source.

The Puritans, by insisting on simplicity in style and form, also forced artists to come to terms with essentials. Early Americans had to create for themselves, because it was so hard to get things from someone else. The average trip from Europe took from five to six weeks, and European goods were prohibitively expensive. It was also almost impossible to come under the domination of fads or fashions. Without affluence, taste had to be more authentic. Neither fad, nor pomposity, nor shoddiness, could be supported. For those were the days before magazines, and before rapid transportation—walking days when people saw things.

Puritanism was the world's most worldly religion. They had an errand in the wilderness, because they thought of America as the land God had given them. They saw themselves as stewards of the plenty and abundance that was all around them. They, and their sons and daughters, with hard work to be sure, proceeded to create a theology that was a celebration of nature. In thankfulness they saw the poetry of the commonplace and the mysteries of the ordinary. They took from that land a heritage that still can be America's. Because they owned the land, culture was theirs in a more personal way than had ever before been possible. The cultural heritage became the common possession of all who were interested. With ownership came careful consideration of purchase. Taste became more authentic and more personal.

The art of the early Americans also follows Kurt Vonnegut's coal mine theory of the arts. A canary is kept in every mine. Very sensitive to gases, it is overcome before poisonous gas can get to the miners, or an explosion can take place. It is thus an early warning system. He suggests that in the same way an artist should be an early warning system for society. And that's what he was in the colonial culture. He showed not only what was obvious in nature and in life, but that which was deep and below the surface. In other words, he permitted his audience and viewers to see all there was to see.

The Individual Made Music

Music was a personal and not a performing art in the first culture. The individual was the maker of music, not merely a listener. However, it has always been difficult to write intelligibly about music, because it is pure in itself and needs no commentary. It is equally difficult to write about the impact of music—to comment on that which cannot be communicated linquistically. For this reason more than any other, there is almost no material on which to base a musical history of the nation's revolutionary period. We have knowledge that folk music of the American Indian existed, but little record of its content. There was a significant amount of music in the colonial village, but most compositions have not survived.

The performers of American music in the first culture were members of the family or neighborhood groups. When Washington was inaugurated less than 10% of the small population lived in cities with a population over 8,000. With no centers for the performing arts, music appreciation grew at the village level. We have evidence of homemade and imported musical instruments dating from the 17th century, of an occasional passage in a journal or diary, of folk tunes that cannot be traced either to Europe or any other source, and of the music played in the church.

The Wesleyan revival of hymn singing had its effects on America. John and Charles Wesley gave Biblical lyrics to the beer hall and tavern tunes of their time, transforming all church music. George Whitefield brought their influence to America, promoting the more formal hymns of Isaac Watts as well. In the period of the village culture, the development of music can best be traced by a study of worship. Progressively, there was more harmony and rhythm, a more lively beat and tempo, and a greater degree of congregational participation. Church choirs were the first organizations to perform classical music in America. Providing a place for nurturing musical talent and appreciation, they gave the most important concerts heard in the period. Choir masters and church organists were the earliest composers.

The colonial home also had an important musical tradition. Virginals, spinets and harpsichords were shipped to the colonies as early as the mid-17th century, according to inventories, diaries and advertisements. By the mid-18th century, many advertisements show that all musical instruments available in England could be purchased in the colonies.

The Lonely Colonists Loved Music

The musical accomplishments of the home were impressive. As instruments became available, instructors were found in most villages. Instruments were purchased directly from England, in the cities of the colonies, or from traveling Yankee pedlars. As early as 1716, Edward Eustace, a Boston organist, advertised in the *Boston News-Letter:* "This is to give notice that there is lately come over from England a choice collection of Instruments, consisting of Flageolets, Flutes, Haut-boys, Bass-Viols, Violins, Bows, Strings, Reeds for Haut-boys."

The lonely colonialists loved music. Every village had two or three homes with major instruments. The children of the wealthy were given instruction in one or more instruments, and taught to sing. There were teachers in almost every village for pianoforte, harpsichord, flute, drums and violin. Bands were formed. There was dancing in the taverns, and fiddling contests at fairs on the green. Concerts in the home are frequently mentioned in diaries and journals.

Soon after 1750, Americans began to manufacture their own instruments, often adding improvements and innovations. Many musical instruments in the village were home designed and homemade, after models available in the cities. Benjamin Franklin invented and made an instrument he called an armonica, which produced music by hemispherical glasses, while others instituted many improvements on traditional instruments. By 1829, when figures became available, more than 2,500 pianos were manufactured in the United States each year.

The first American composer to make music his vocation was William Billings. He began composing in 1765. Five years later he produced *The New England Psalm Singer*, and announced his musical declaration of independence from the chafing restrictions of primitive simplicity in psalm tunes and hymns. For, as he proclaimed in a later work, he was determined to make "powerful" music instead of the "old slow tunes." His composition, "Jargon," is considered the first piece of modern composition, a prelude to Schoenberg and Stravinsky.

It was in the nature of the American character to try to make music representational. Jean Gehot wrote an impressive Overture in twelve movements, relating his experience sailing from England to America. The subjects of the movements are revealing: affectionate separation from their friends, going on board, preparation for sailing, a storm, a calm, universal joy on seeing land, and thanksgiving for a safe arrival. Together, the work of Billings and Gehot preview the compositions of Charles Ives.

A Lively Village Culture

During the first culture there was only a narrow division between popular and classical music. Most performers were able to move easily from one to the other. In an age before phonograph records, all music was "live." An astounding variety was in evidence within every community.

Songs which became popular did so for their subject matter—patriotic, humorous or sentimental—or for their melody, or their beat. Songs like "Yankee-Doodle," "Hail Columbia," or even "The Star Spangled Banner" were not conceived as anthems, but as expressions of patriotic and nationalistic zeal. Both for their setting and the stirring emotional empathy which they elicit, these songs live for every new generation. Particularly impressive by current standards is Smith's "America," which neither by association nor text is connected with war. It states simply, albeit romantically, America's hopes and blessings.

While patriotic songs are always interesting, their worth as music is generally recognized as slight. Light music of entertainment and sectional folk music, however, often grow out of the finest musical traditions. No American composer of classical music had greater gifts or more originality than Stephen Foster. A master of melody as well as light verse, he captured the recreational mood of the village. "Oh! Susanna," "Old Folks at Home," "My Old Kentucky Home," and "De Camptown Races" are still sung with gusto and warmth. The light ballads of the period gave to music a more crucial part in family life, than it was to have in later years. The village culture was a dancing, singing, lively affair, in which beat and rhythm were felt.

The mechanical age was not able to affect the world of music with the same stifling quickness, with which it gripped other art forms, because new immigrants kept the musical heritage continually alive. Classical music was considered part of the necessary inheritance of every educated person. A far higher percentage of the population studied some form of music seriously in the colonial period, than do so today.

Pumpkin Yellow Buildings

From the beginning, the very process of American

building showed artistic integrity. Many structures were indeed works of art. The colonial home had many of modern architecture's values—functional design, a clearing away of needless detail, no fake effects, integrity of materials, an emphasis on texture, integration of color and form, the use of light and shadow, mutual involvement of user and designer, an expression of craftsmanship, and a combination of strength and warmth.

Fortunately for those early buildings, nails were costly and scarce, and most homes were closely fitted and built without the use of iron. Wood was used, and it made a better fastener than nails, for it could expand and contract. The framing, exposed and massive, records for us today the patient process of erecting secure structures. Oak was the wood most often used. The marks of the hewing are still visible, as is the careful craftsmanship at the joints. Fitted together by the joining of tenon and mortise, they have the beauty of sculpture. Only at the beginning of the eighteenth century did power sawing supplant hewing.

Shingles, clapboards and siding were the early American's first defense against the weather, and a wooden floor was added as soon as affluence, time and ability would allow. However, in their beginnings, many of the colonial homes had plain floors of pounded dirt, which had to be swept smooth each day. There are records of elaborate designs traced in these dirt carpets, to brighten the home for holidays and festive occasions.

Contrary to what most people think, exteriors of the first buildings were as likely to be painted red or pumpkin yellow as white. A new meeting house in Pomfret, Connecticut had a coat of bright yellow paint on it. Another church was painted a vivid orange, trimmed with a warm chocolate color. Originality in color and in color combinations was commonplace. The impression of the completed frame of the colonial structure was one of boundless strength, of steadfastness, and of sculptured beauty.

In most villages there were one or two examples of Georgian architecture. Built during the Federal period after the Revolution in a mood of wealth and aristocracy, these homes were in reality, the village museums and status symbols within the community.

The builder used handbooks for many details—the cornices, moldings, windows and interior decoration. Lighting considerations were of crucial importance. Often there was a fine fan-light window above the front doorway, and windows in the upper story had monitor tops to allow light into the attic. The finest of these homes had richly patterned and imported wallpapers, many prints and paintings on the walls, needlepoint, fire poles, perhaps a Grandfather's Clock on an impressive stairway, and paneling and carvings to go with the high ceilings.

Many homes, even the simplest, had decorative wall paintings, hand painted chimney boards and fireboards, showing a general thirst for beauty in the people who lived in them. When wallpaper came to the simpler homes, it brought a brightness to the dark walls. And it should be pointed out here that eighteenth century wallpaper was nothing like today's commercial product. Colonial wallpaper was the product of artists and artisans who carefully reproduced designs by hand. It can better be compared to the sizable lithographs of twentieth century artists.

The home was the center of life for the people of the colonial village. It was the place of work and recreation, of learning and communication, of sleeping and eating. A villager lived most of his life within a ten-mile radius of his farm, and except for church and tavern, the lifestyle of the people was developed almost exclusively in the home.

Poor Furniture Didn't Survive

Almost every object in a colonial home was

carefully chosen. Little wealth was available for expenditure on non-essentials. And by necessity, life was spent in intimate relationship with these objects. In the days before motivational research and advertising pressure, possessions represented a self-conscious value judgment. A man's possessions were likely to be truly representative of his essential character.

First among these objects in the colonial home was, of course, furniture. And no art form has such an intimate relationship with people. Unlike architecture, it is portable, and with it the first colonists began a process which never ended. They imported or brought furniture with them from the home country. This established a constant competition between the native craftsman and the foreign supplier. It meant that style and craftsmanship in furniture underwent a far more rapid development and decline than was the case in architecture.

No single American art form has as many 17th and 18th century examples of excellence available for twentieth century study. Unlike architecture, where coincidences of location and function indiscriminately destroy or preserve both the vulgar and the excellent, the poorest furniture does not usually survive. Finer materials and excellent craftsmanship make the best pieces more durable. In addition, objects of highest quality are usually cared for better in this period. Scholars believe that styles in furniture persistently evolved toward the excellence of simplicity.

No effort was made to fill the early homes with furniture, since space had its own integrity. Stools, chests, bed frames and trestle tables completed the usual furniture inventory. In addition, most families used hand-shaped wooden dishes.

The craftsmanship represented was "soundly medieval." But as labor was scarce, and since all could have land of their own, it was increasingly difficult to persuade the early craftsman to stay in his craft and work for others. Those who did remain could not find apprentices. Even after the term of service was shortened, boys were hard to find. While the master-craftsman in England could demand an "apprentice-piece" to safeguard the excellence of workmanship, American craftsmen were not able to maintain any such standard. But over a long period of time, this same fact also insured high standards, for the new system encouraged creativity, innovation and excellence, by making each man responsible for his own work. The new craftsman was free from controlling influence early in his career. He was forced quickly to adapt to new materials, and original usages. And, most important of all, he had to display real competence, in order to convince the customer he would not be just as well off doing the work himself.

In our colonial beginnings, homespun linen, spreads, and hangings filled the hope chests of young girls, who spent their adolescence perfecting their home-making ability. We call these artisans amateurs, but the time they spent giving design and color to the fabric which they made from raw wool or flax, makes any such designation unfair. Almost all designs endlessly produced today evolve from those earlier times. An entire population took responsibility for design, which gave it many more possibilities for creativity, than is possible when a limited number of professionals are in charge.

The Wonder of New Shapes

Most of the utensils, dishes, spoons and buckets used by the early settlers were beautifully formed in wood, by men who knew the mysterious wonder of new shapes and fine grains. These tools and utensils shaped from wood were lighter, better balanced, and better designed than their European counterparts. Each piece was unique. But because the work was so slow, the public needed another substance to take its

73

place after 1700. While the wooden trencher remained in use throughout the 18th century, pewter became the general substitute. The pewterer made jugs, tankards, teapots, dishes of all sizes, cups, pitchers, bowls, lamps, utensils, door latches, candlestick holders, and hundreds of other objects of art. Churches extended this art, by ordering communion ware, baptismal bowls, and plates. Because it was relatively expensive, pewter was meticulously cared for, shined and decorated.

In the New England area, crafts were given additional stimulus by the climate. People had to stay indoors during hard weather, and the infertility of the land encouraged other pursuits. Time, the priceless ingredient in all art, was available.

From the earliest days in America, the goldsmith and the silversmith were one, working in the most precious metals, and achieving designs of intricate beauty. The work was painstakingly slow, demanding craftsmanship of a timeless quality. The first design influences were French—Rococo and Classic. Later, Chinese and Arab motifs and the forms of the Greek revival became important. Silversmiths relied on the various handbooks on architecture for their inspiration, and the craft's development paralleled that of architecture.

That the craftsman was a generalist is supported by the career of Paul Revere, a noted silversmith. A versatile craftsman, he cast bronze bells and cannon, engraved prints, made tin and false teeth, was a printer, jeweler, framer, and blacksmith.

The American Eagle, Bird of Many Parts

Folk art was used to decorate many of the everyday implements of life. The eagle, the most common symbol of the young republic, was subjected to hundreds of stylistic interpretations. The popular taste did not allow the bird to solidify into one single form. Alternating in interpretation between friendliness and fierceness, peace and war, artists used the eagle to state the American paradox.

Paintings by Americans have always reflected two contrasting forces—native genius influenced by the awesome power of the land, and professional training reflecting the roots of European civilization. While European painting was controlled by those individuals and institutions which gave patronate—Royalty and the Church—colonial painting was done in response to the artist's inspiration or commercial speculation. Standards of craftsmanship declined, but originality of interpretation substantially increased.

Art a Secular Concern

Since there were few wealthy patrons in America, artists could reflect their own personal values and individual aims. However, they were also subject to a public taste and fashion not known in Europe. Since any man with enough money could commission a portrait or purchase a landscape, the artist had to satisfy a great variety of requests. Before mass communications, no universal style was possible. In Europe, Royal and ecclesiastical patrons kept art the province of the aristocracy. In America, individual patrons in the village society eventually gave it to the masses. Primitive American artists were not greatly appreciated in Europe, because artistic excellence had been confused with beauty. It remained for the most contemporary of twentieth century American artists, to rediscover the importance of colonial folk art.

In the beginnings of this nation, without illustrated papers or magazines, without great cathedrals, without great private collections, and without significant institutional interest or control, painting came to be authentically personal for both the artist and the community. The loss of the "aesthetically sophisticated client" gave the painter individual freedom of expression. He could go directly to nature for his subjects. In the escape from the predetermined subject matter of church and state, color, form and function came to the surface. In America, art quickly became a secular concern.

The first painters worked under great difficulty, their materials were primitive, and they often ground their own paint and made their own brushes. Professionally made tools took months to arrive from Europe, and even then had to be selected by others. The necessity of developing and making materials and supplies through technological experimentation, resulted in a constant improvement of both paints and tools.

Also Some of the Worst Painting

The first craft painters were called limners, a word derived from the French "luminaire" meaning to light up or illuminate that which is dark. And the early portrait painters did indeed have the job of brightening the form and character of their solemn subjects. They succeeded with impressive regularity. A lack of fine clothing, jewelry and ornamentation focused attention upon the character of the subject itself, allowing American portrait painting to be less formal and more interesting than English work of the same time.

However, some of the worst painting in the history of art also gained wallspace in many colonial homes. The customer, who had only the trade and tavern signs with which to compare his portrait, was often uncritically satisfied with a bland, repetitious likeness. The painter also often flattered him with finer clothing and finer facial features than he possessed.

Amid a mass of good, bad and mediocre painting, a fullness of style slowly emerged. Some of the more ambitious early limners arranged subjects into groups. They surrounded them with symbols of authority or occupation, and gave them backgrounds with landscapes or elegant furnishings and attempted to show depth of character, as well as a likeness. An unusually expressive portrait was done of Anne Pollard in 1721, when she is said to have been over one hundred years of age. The former tavern keeper had more than one hundred and thirty descendants, and was the last survivor of the settlers of Boston. She claimed to be the first person to come ashore, and the first citizen of the city. The artist, not content with literal realism, tried to capture her entire life in one portrait. He put into it the arrogance and delight of one who outlived all her contemporaries, and the brittle toughness of one who knew her claims could no longer be challenged. This picture has within itself the weaknesses and the strengths of early American portraiture. Technically, it is justly faulted, but it is one of the first impressionistic works, presenting not only what the painter "saw" but "all there was to see." The roughness of early American painting, fully explained by the training and environment of native artists, does not prevent its quiet power from exhibiting itself. This strength was often lacking in English portraits of the same period. By establishing a self-conscious identity for an entire people in the years following the Revolution, the portraitists lifted their trade into the center of a developing culture.

The landscape school of painting was the first original American movement. It began during the Revolution, when Ralph Earl turned from the limited format of portrait painting to local settings, landscapes and historical events. His historical paintings of the Revolution and other heroic subjects, started a school which continued for a century. Earl was also one of the first to paint the natural wonders of the country, including Niagara Falls.

West's Mythological Paintings

In painting, Americans combined an expression of

the spirit of the nation and the spiritual depth of the individual artist. Great art began to appear, and in a little less than two centuries, a tradition emerged. Samuel F. B. Morse, who died in the last quarter of the nineteenth century, was a student of Benjamin West, the first outstanding figure in American artistic history.

Born in 1718, West is more important for the works he inspired than for his own artistic achievement. Almost every important painter of the time was helped by West. His own paintings were elaborate mythological interpretations on massive canvasses filled with classic figures, which were insufferably melodramatic. West's figures were idealized to a degree which is now humorous. Even Biblical themes became story-telling monstrosities.

But those with enough genius and talent were able to use his technical help, and to appreciate his efforts to be a bridge over which old world influence traveled to the new. As President of the British Academy and the friend of King George III, West had both the wealth and the power to aid young Americans. He was primarily an agent of popular taste, and not of the forces of reaction. As a romantic who believed art should represent and illustrate ideal cultural forces, his professional advice bred an eclecticism which inhibited the natural talents of many young Americans. He taught them to think and paint like Europeans. They were led away from authentic experience toward false sophistication. They became too willing to copy because commercial success demanded conformity.

The greatest of early American artists, John Singleton Copley, illustrates both the grandeur of American art, and the debilitating effects of continental sophistication. Most scholars agree that Copley did his best and most original work before he went to London. As a possessor of innovative and discriminating talent, he had a brief five-year period of training, using as study material, prints and original paintings and copies brought to America by John Smibert. His earliest portraits show a clear mastery of painting techniques. He was able to portray lace and finery, shade and color, light and shadow. Copley also gave life to real people. His portrait of Jacob Fowle speaks volumes about the patrician environment, cultivated by colonial aristocrats. The gun he carries is for the hunt, yet the subject's eye shows he would be free to use it against a foe. Copley's miniatures and full length portraits are of equal excellence. He painted hands as expressive of character as faces, demonstrating the technical proficiency of his art.

"Nathaniel Hurd" (1765), and "Boy with Squirrel" (1765), are two of the finest examples of his full artistic power. An intense personal style overwhelms the particular subject matter. Here is no photographic realism. His selective eye has focused not on object or subject, but upon a specific mood, a particular moment of life. The style is spare, simple, precise, pure. The young artist made spiritual statements in his paintings. In his two versions of "Watson and the Shark," Copley was one of the first to bring the viewer into the painting, allowing his response to become part of the total artistic experience. Terror, shock, wonder, and sympathy, became genuine responses to the drama and power of his work.

Charles Willson Peale and other members of the Peale family, continued the tradition of interpretative realism. Gilbert Stuart, the professional's professional, who concentrated on heads and faces, tried to portray the character of those who made a revolution. Smibert, Joseph Badger, Joseph Blackburn, Robert Feke, John Trumbull, and Thomas Sully shared with many others in the development of a profession.

American Folk Art In the Vanguard

At the same time, the period following the

revolution inspired the most exciting expressions of folk art in American history. Winthrop Chandler, Mary Ann Willson, Rufus Porter, and many others now nameless, knew neither rules nor convention. They had in their work many of the effects now so admired in modern art—exploitation of pure and arbitrary colors; distortions of point of view, scale, time, form and mass; use of composite portrayals of space, sequence, design and tone; and integration of dreams, symbols, myths and reality.

They escaped from the limits of the frame, and from the conventions of their time. Space and time did not control either theme or structure. Their art reflects the tempo and the lifestyle of the village, in ways even the most technically brilliant portrait misses. The dimensions of wholeness and spiritual depth were evident in what they attempted, and even at times in what they achieved.

Trips to Shelburne, Vermont; Sturbridge, Massachusetts; Williamsburg, Virginia; or Dearborn, Michigan, will show the reader the great depth of these primitive masters. At Sturbridge, there is a portrait of a Dr. Smith of Mount Vernon, New York. It reveals a low level of craftsmanship at the same time as it presents a high level of interpretive power. The doctor's instruments are on a table, suspended in space, seemingly on the verge of falling to the floor. While the artist ignored careful representation, he allowed us to "see" the limitations of these medical implements, and the frustrations involved in their use. Through the window there is a corner of the doctor's village. His character then is the subject of the painting, not his image. The same artist, E. Woolson, has a companion painting of Mrs. Smith at Sturbridge. She is seen in her domestic setting with sewing implements and other symbols, which focus on the responsibilities of motherhood.

At these living museums the visitor can also see the creative use of a whole variety of media. On display are radiant portraits on glass and boards, and charcoal sketches on sandpaper which show a keen appreciation of texture, not seen before the contemporary collage. Fireboards and over-mantels possess the same textured strength. Theorem painting on velvet, silhouettes and shadow pictures, paintings on window shades and wallboards, and on old paneling, show a spirit of experimentation. Even if economically motivated, these speak to the fullness of life of the early Americans. In the colonial village, art furnished a good part of the excitement. The entire community responded to a new creation. All had to see, all were curious, and all felt personal involvement.

The Webb Art Gallery in Shelburne gives an overview of early landscape painting. Most of the finest artists of one of the world's first schools of landscape painting, are represented in this single collection: Thomas Doughty, Frederick Church, Thomas Cole, Albert Bierstadt, Thomas Chambers, E. C. Coates, Daniel Huntington, Asher B. Durand, T. P. Rossiter, Frederick Rondel, Fitz Hugh Land, and Seth Eastman.

The American Impressionists

For the first time in the history of art, nature—which has always been the basic source of design—became the subject itself. The process of development can be traced: first a man had his portrait painted, then he wanted a view of his house and grounds. His horizon then broadened to include his neighborhood and the village square, and finally famous landmarks and national wonders. Landscapes were especially popular as subjects for murals in public meeting places, taverns, ballrooms, Masonic Halls, churches and government buildings. This work was not art for art's sake, but an honest attempt to convey the overwhelming importance of the abundant land in American life. From the land came the myths, the legends, the wealth, and the power of the new nation. American writers—Emerson, Thoreau, Hawthorne and Melville—were doing with words what the painters were attempting with brushes—providing an inner view of the meaning of life in this land. Some assumptions, of course, proved unfortunate—especially the tendency to identify virtue with nature. For a few, there developed a dichotomy between America's people and her precious landscape.

Predating the impressionists by a decade, George Inness painted out-of-doors. Inness was, in many respects, the most complete artist of his time. Traveling in Europe in 1847, he studied in London and Rome. His Swedenborgian theology encouraged him to see his art as a vehicle of spiritual and emotional conversion. As the first self-confessed impressionist, Inness brought a mystical depth to much of his work. His teaching is of great importance, for it offered a constructive alternative to the then developing culture of the mechanical age—an alternative firmly rejected later by his fellow Americans. As a consequence, Paris and the French Impressionists remained the hub of the art world for another century instead of the American school. Inness wrote: "The purpose of the painter is simply to reproduce in other minds the impression which a scene has made upon him. A work of art does not appeal to the intellect. It does not appeal to the moral sense. Its aim is not to instruct, not to edify, but to awaken an emotion . . . It must be a single emotion if the work has unity, as every such work should have, and the true beauty of the work consists in the beauty of the sentiment or emotion which it inspires. Its real greatness consists in the quality and force of this emotion."

America also has a strong heritage of genre painting—perhaps because of the richness of its primitive tradition. These story-telling, anecdotal, completely personal paintings show the changing times. In the years following 1790, this kind of painting was fresh, original, and completely intro-spective.

Hicks Had the Free Gift of Grace

Another interesting aspect of art in colonial times was how the really good painter surfaced. For one thing, as villages and towns multiplied after the Revolution, society became inbred. Each villager was valued for himself, and even for his eccentricity. The country artist, almost always self-taught, was asked to paint these villagers and the society in which they lived. More often than not these artisans were medio-cre in both inspiration and talent.

However, occasionally one of the thousand villages would contain a man of real genius, in whose hands painting came alive, and whose work offered a natu-ralism which infused his awareness into a moment of time. One of the most important was the Quaker, Edward Hicks. While the villagers ridiculed him for his religious beliefs and for his eccentric habits, his work was a powerful statement of the richness of his mind. He wanted to expand his art to include God's revelation, His world and His people. Hicks' paintings survive in good condition, because he gained a tech-nical mastery of his medium in his early training as a house and sign painter. His favorite subject was "William Penn's Treaty With the Indians," for he felt the need to communicate the values of peace and security in a world of violent temperament, already beginning to be intruded upon by impersonal ma-chines. He thought of "Penn's Holy Experiment" as an extension and fulfillment of Isiah's prophecy: "The wolf also shall dwell with the lamb, and the leopard shall lie down with the kid; and the calf and the young lion and the fatling together; and a little child shall lead them." (Isaiah 11:6).

Hicks painted nearly one hundred individual inter-pretations of "The Peaceable Kingdom." Following the animal list given in Isaiah, he put all beasts of the field together in an effort to show the pervasive power of love. "The Cornell Farm," a masterpiece, captures the flavor of life in the rural American village. It is an exercise in geometric design, which speaks both of life as it is, and of life as it ought to be. Hicks is close to the spirit of Pieter Bruegel. He brings to his painting the same seriousness and joy in the interpretation of metaphysical themes. Any difference is in tone. While Bruegel enters into the power of the demonic, Hicks has been captured by the free gift of grace, which brings security and peace, through the pastoral care of a living savior.

William Sidney Mount, Washington Allston, David G. Blythe, and George Caleb Bingham, were others who found poetry in the life and character of field-hands, tavern keepers, fishermen, river boatmen, farmers, musicians, and dancers.

Historian—Painter of Indian Tribes

Another type of genre painting in the nation's early years portrayed the country's self-discovery. Self-taught and willing to follow the road west, George Catlin became the self-appointed historian of Indian tribes and frontier settlements. He lived six years with the western tribes, recording their native customs. His paintings of war dances, buffalo hunts, exotic ceremonies, and natural wonders are living history. In a brief period he finished more than one hundred paintings, including many of his most famous works.

It is currently fashionable to depreciate Catlin's efforts, because of his many technical faults and because of his subject matter. Yet his art has an authentic style, and communicates America's cultural heritage in a unique way. The great amount of his work—over six hundred oil paintings of western life and thousands of sketches—made an uneven quality inevitable. His method of work, the only one possible in the circumstances, makes such an accomplishment miraculous. Throughout most of each year, he lived with a tribe, making drawings of subjects he found interesting. In the winter months he made finished paintings from the drawings. Such diligence produced an historical vision which is still the best portrayal of all aspects of the life of the West—of the violent, mobile and rough, as well as the quiet and peaceful.

An even greater artist in this genre painting of national discovery, was James John Audubon, who chose the birds and animals of the continent as his subjects. More artist than scientist, he showed a genius for dramatic setting, and a remarkable ability as a colorist and draftsman. In one of the most ambitious and successful projects in the history of art, he powerfully illuminates the natural life of the new world. The great bird pictures were issued in parts from 1827 to 1838. Within a quarter of a century of their completion, such a project would have been impossible because man was changing the landscape and its inhabitants. Audubon often reveals more artistic skill in his portraits of birds and animals, than did contemporary portrait painters.

The painters of the first culture knew that art could never be completely sufficient unto itself. They were successful, not because a native genius had been developed, but because they were honest individuals possessing spirit and a cause, which carried over into their work. They had a new world to reveal—to themselves first—and only secondarily to others. The Puritan's aversion to prettiness and sentimentality brought a strength of life reflected in his art. In the first culture the mere representation of reality was not considered art. The lifestyle of the people demanded a more vigorous, deeper interpretation of life.

The Literature of an Abundant Land

American writers of the first culture extended this

honesty into words. Their writing was of self-discovery in the medieval tradition. It was produced primarily for self-satisfaction. Writing primarily because they felt a need to express themselves, the outstanding authors had the integrity of those who record their thoughts without any motivation of popular prestige or commercial success.

In the nineteenth century, American writers who could take their place in the literary history of the western world began to appear. Popular favorites like Nathaniel Parker Willis, Washington Irving, James Fenimore Cooper, and Mrs. Sigourney were not unlike other successful practitioners of the craft in any age. But in the background, three men set their own standards, dealing with experiences at many levels, forging styles which were superior to the limitations of their time. Edgar Allan Poe, Nathaniel Hawthorne, and Herman Melville conserved the novel as an art form until the early years of the twentieth century, when Joyce, Kafka, Faulkner and others reclaimed its usefulness, while others used the form only as an exercise in romantic escape. In their hands the novel became a probe of human existence—an anti-environmental medium. They spent little time on philosophical theory, except when it advanced the story line. But all three explored new territory, as they delved into free form imagination, changing perceptions, macabre humor, the mystery in immediate experience, and a questioning of the alleged moralities of civilization.

Poe Challenges Mechanical Age

Edgar Allan Poe (1809-1849), clearly the most lucid of the three, did not accomplish any one substantial masterwork upon which a career may be judged. In hundreds of short stories, articles, poems and reviews, however, he demonstrated an obvious genius. A brilliant linguist whose fascination was in style, form and rhythm, Poe gave attention to the sounds of words, achieving effects through alliteration and internal rhyme. His gift of imagination is constantly underplayed in the building rhythm of his tales. He is the first great artistic outsider, in a tradition which now includes Dostoevsky, Ibsen, Kafka, Camus, Hesse, and many twentieth century American masters. Poe presented the self as outcast, as he dealt with the mind and the soul, with probing words of passion.

He was also the first to challenge the mechanical age. He saw its impotence, and not its power. All the themes on this subject, now so common, are first seen in Poe. He developed the anti-hero, was cynical about patriotism, and felt threatened by the inhumanity of industry. He understood the loss of identity, the feelings of insecurity, the despair of hopelessness, and the multiplicity of corruption in material success. Poe's style captured truth by indirection. The meaning of his tales is evident only to those who know the paradoxical, ironical, symbolic, ambiguous and proximate nature of truth. As meaning is buried in creation, so it is deep beneath the surface of his work, occasionally illuminated by metaphors and narrative, but ever waiting for the contribution of the observer.

Poe was the first to correlate all the senses into a single sensory response. Using combinations of words which made visceral and auditory demands on the reader, he was able to communicate a sense of tactile awareness, of smell and taste. As he developed what is called synesthesia, or the production of sensation in one part of the body by a stimulus applied to another part, Poe created images which impressed themselves upon the subconscious. His characters are tuned to all levels of awareness. Symbolic images draw empathic responses from the reader. Poe had the gift of allowing his readers the privilege of seeing themselves in his characters. The musicality of his poetry elicits a mood response.

Poe believed that the demonic forces of evil which bring man to tragedy, are only temporarily avoided through a combination of common sense and circumstance. Any real solution comes not objectively in experience, but internally in the spirit of the human being. He invented the modern forms of science fiction and the detective story, and was one of the first literary artists to be deeply interested in science, and willing to attempt scientific themes. In *The Balloon Hoax,* he tells the story of a flyer, Monck Mason, who flies in a balloon with eight passengers from Wales to South Carolina in 75 hours. Reprinting the story as if it were fact, he was able to perpetuate a hoax similar in effect to the Orson Welles' "Men from Mars" radio broadcast a century later. In *The Unparalleled Adventure of One Hans Pfaall* he anticipates, with considerable detail and invention, the flight to the moon, which took place 134 years later. He shows dimensions for mankind in such a step that the astronauts seemed to have missed. He is able to break the hold of time sequence looking ahead into the future in *Mellonta Tauta,* and far back into the past in *Some Words With A Mummy.* The rhythms inherent in his poetry and his prose communicated a deeper understanding of the process of nature and of the humanity of life, than any other work of his time. What some reviewers saw as a sexless morbidity is, in reality, an open embrace of the abyss resulting in a willingness to see the self as the stranger and the world as beset by a plague.

Rich Background in New England History

Nathaniel Hawthorne (1804-1864), the second great author who has modern significance, was the son of a sea captain who died when his boy was only four. Nathaniel's mother immediately retreated to her room on the second floor of the family home, where she remained in absolute seclusion for forty years.

Craftsmanship was the foundation of the first culture. Since everyone was a generalist and could form things for themselves, the craftsman had to be exceptionally able to get any trade at all.

Time, the priceless ingredient in all art and craftsmanship, was available in the first culture.

Emerson wrote: "I am only an experimenter . . . I unsettle all things.
No facts are to me sacred: none are profane: I simply experiment, an
endless seeker, with no part at my back."

As the governmental process moved farther from the people the system
of capitalism was corrupted as the powerful received special treatment.

Jenny Lind

This 1850 engraving of Jenny Lind, one of the first stars, marks the beginning of the spectator interest in the arts. Music was a personal, not a performing art, in the first culture.

FRANKLIN'S PRINTING PRESS.

FAUST'S FIRST PROOF FROM MOVEABLE TYPE.

"A direct relationship between the work done and a finished product was harder and harder to perceive." These contemporary prints are what happened to the printing industry in less than fifty years. The media starts becoming the message. Mechanical improvements gave rapid reproduction possibilities, thus forcing authors to abbreviate both article length and research time.

This 1851 engraving by W. T. Peters portrays the family centered life style of the first culture.

The solid, majestic park bank symbolizes the new view of property conceived in the Mechanical Age. In the first culture all property was clearly visible in the community. With banks, the limits of "success" were constantly multiplied and never defined.

After a period of escape to Bowdoin College in Maine, Hawthorne returned to Salem where he lived for twelve years in his mother's shadow. His existence was that of an unintentional recluse, finding light only as he created art.

Suddenly, without apparent reason, he decided to socialize, to mix with his own kind. He befriended all the literary giants of the time: Longfellow, Emerson, Thoreau, Margaret Fuller, and Melville. A shy stranger in the busy world of industrial and national expansion, in his literary art he chose to develop themes dealing with cultural and moral conflicts while he earned his living in business and civil service. New England history offered him rich background material for his writing. One of the first to feel that anguish which would be characteristically American, Hawthorne dealt directly with the guilt, doubt, and shallowness so commonplace at the dawn of the mechanical age. In the years between 1820 and 1850 a transformation took place, and Hawthorne reflected on the happening. From this personal background and a fear of melancholia, came the themes of many of his stories. He created lonely, recluse people who were by circumstance separated from their own humanity. The clarity of his work was more dependent upon style, than on either logical sequence or intellectual conformity. Able to treat the most mundane theme with fresh insight, Hawthorne dealt in powerful feelings, with little more than a hint of sentimentality. He was most appreciated by his fellow artists. Poe gave him his first important recognition by understanding his intent and relating it to the changing culture. Also, Melville was slightly overwhelmed by cultural patriotism when he wrote in *Hawthorne and His Moses:* "Now I do not say that Nathaniel of Salem is a greater man than William of Avon, or as great. But the difference between the two men is by no means immeasurable. Not a very great deal more and Nathaniel was verily William."

A Veil on Every Face

With the publication of *Twice-Told Tales* in 1837, Hawthorne's status as the most intellectually interesting American author of the nineteenth century was established. One of the tales, "The Minister's Black Veil," is a vivid commentary on the many levels upon which life may be lived. On the eve of his wedding a minister puts on a black veil which he refuses to discard. His fiancee abandons him, and his life becomes one of disillusionment and morbid meditation. His parishioners, threatened by his gloom, reject him. Just before his death he sees a veil on every face, and he is finally buried in his own black veil. The story is typical of Hawthorne, in that it poses many more questions than it answers. The deeply symbolic mood of the story grants the reader the privilege of his own interpretation.

More philosophical intrigue is found in the tale of "The Ambitious Guest," the story of a youth spending the night in the wilderness of the White Mountains, as the guest of a simple family who keep a trailside cottage. He frankly states his dream for fame, fortune, and happiness. His ambition is contrasted with the simpler wishes of the household. A great landslide brings death to all the same night. Is this story a commentary on the Manifest Destiny America was then struggling to achieve, or upon the image of personal success envisioned by the characters, or just a statement on the finite character of man? As a contemporary of the great Danish theologian Sören Kierkegaard, Hawthorne had much the same intensity of spirit and existential concern. His greatest works show a similar approach to life and death.

A Hundred Years Before Camus

The Scarlet Letter is rich in symbolism, with a

Faustian bargain at the center of the story. The main character, Hester, learns to live with her sin of adultery. By accepting herself and devoting her life to the wider community, she shows the irrelevance of the moralisms of the mechanical age. Judgments are held less important than facts in a complex world. The theme of the novel is not adultery, but the effect of sin on the rationality, the beliefs, and the lives of the major characters. The scarlet letter becomes a badge, not of a sinful act, but of the condition of all human beings. The individual stands guilty before God, estranged and dependent. Chillingsworth, the most self-esteemed character, is revealed as the sinner who handles his guilt through hate. Although Dimmesdale, the seemingly holy clergyman, confesses his guilt publicly, all are equally scarred at the conclusion of the novel. Avoiding the temptation to moralize, Hawthorne, a hundred years before Camus, wrote the story of a modern anti-hero.

The House of Seven Gables is even more directly related to the twentieth century. The house was a symbol of a civilization which had fallen into decay. Its occupants clung to hereditary fortunes which had lost their value. The young reformer wanted to get rid of the past in the name of a sovereign present: "If each generation were allowed and expected to build its own houses, that single change, comparatively unimportant in itself, would imply every reform which society is now suffering for. . . . Shall we never, never get rid of this past? It lies upon the present like a giant's dead body. In fact, the case is just as if a young giant were compelled to waste all his strength in carrying about the corpse of the old giant, who died a long while ago and only needs to be decently buried . . . A dead man sits on all our judgment seats; and living judges do not but search out and repeat his decisions. We read in dead men's books. We laugh at dead men's jokes and cry at dead men's pathos, and die of the same remedies with which dead doctors killed their patients. We worship the living deity according to dead men's forms and creeds. Whatever we do of our own free motion, a dead man's icy hand obstructs us. . . ."

Within the novel he used techniques consistent with his theme. Time stands still at the death of the judge, so he can show its tyranny over mankind. The family structure is examined in a review of events—past, present and future—as if they were happening all-at-once. He shows that meaning does not depend upon any time lag. The train ride of Hepzibah and Clifford gives Hawthorne an opportunity to show the interrelationship of space, time, and speed. The ability to lay aside conventional development by logical time sequence, and the freedom to look beyond reason for meaning give this work its unique dimension.

Life in a Whaling Venture

Although he lived until 1891, Herman Melville's best work was completed forty years before his death. At twenty, in order to escape financial difficulties he sought a career at sea, making first a trip to Liverpool aboard the St. Lawrence. He sailed again in 1841 to the South Seas. Deserting his ship, in rapid sequence he lived among cannibals, took a native mistress, participated in a mutiny, became a beachcomber, joined the United States Navy, and visited the Galapagos Islands on his way home around Cape Horn.

His contemporaries could hardly understand the harmonious unity he affected in his work between imagination and reason. Devoid of sentimentality and strongly autobiographical, Melville's prose had all the symbolic depth and creative urgency found in that of Poe and Hawthorne. In addition, he saw a key to meaning in the "wickedness" of the mechanical age.

Moby Dick, dedicated to Hawthorne, is a moral parable which looks at life from the perspective of a whaling adventure. Some have interpreted it as Melville's attempt to reinforce the central doctrines of Christianity. Others see it as another example of his use of the artistic devices of deception, to conceal his actual beliefs. Either way, it is a profound interpretation of human life, its struggle with nature, and its compulsion to define good and evil. The complex symbolism allows the reader to spiritually withdraw from all outward wordly complications. Yet the withdrawal involves living fully each existential moment: "as the swift monster drags you deeper and deeper into the frantic shoal, you bid adieu to circumspect life and only exist in a delirious throb." Life takes its color from the challenges on the razor's edge: "Ahab had cherished a wild vindictiveness against the whale . . . in his frantic morbidness he at last came to identify with him, not only all his bodily woes, but all his intellectual and spiritual exasperations."

Indeed, whaling was a symbol for the entire success ethic. Melville describes "a most surprising success":

Not only had barrels of beef and bread been given away to make room for the far more valuable sperm, . . . even the cabin table itself had been knocked into kindling-wood; and the cabin mess dined off the broad head of an oil-butt, lashed down to the floor for a centerpiece. In the forecastle, the sailors had actually caulked and pitched their chests, and filled them; it was humorously added, that the cook had clapped a head on his largest boiler, and filled it; that the steward had plugged his spare coffeepot and filled it; that the harpooners had headed the sockets of their irons and filled them; that indeed everything was filled with sperm, except the captain's pantaloons pockets, and those he reserved to thrust his hands into, in self-complacent testimony of his entire satisfaction.

Spiritual depth in life is assumed by Melville, even

in the structure of *Moby Dick*. There can be no moral grandeur where there is no morality. Melville wrote of the tragedies of individuals subjected to a world becoming impersonal and fragmented. He recognized both the consequences of mechanization and the shallowness of success.

Pierre, Melville's novel of psychological conflict, is a study of response to the pressures of unmerited success, which dared to attack the clichés of motherhood. All Melville's work, although often bitterly pessimistic, wrestles with basic questions in a manner more typical of a pre-literate culture. Physical and emotional factors predominate over rational and logical ideas. A man can love death as well as life, another man as well as a woman. He refuses to adapt conventional patterns of sequence and consecutiveness of thought, and is free to appeal to all the senses in both the style and substance of his writing.

The Soul and the Machine

By the middle 1850's Melville was sure, as evidenced in *Israel Potter* or *Fifty Years of Exile,* that a once vibrant America was growing stagnant in the grip of the industrial east. He yearned for hope in a still expanding west, without being greatly encouraged. More than any other man of letters, Melville saw the conflict between the soul and the machine. Years before Henry Adams, he created the basic symbols of that conflict.

In the years after the Revolution, America had many important writers of nonfiction, because the entire world was interested in the great experiment. The new adventure of exploration gave stimulus to a new interest in history and travel. After the first generation of settlers had done their work, many recorded their experiences. Bradford and Winthrop, the Mathers, and Jonathan Edwards told of their experience, and their theology. Franklin, Jefferson,

Adams, Paine, and many others, told the story of the Revolution. Washington Irving wrote biographies of Columbus and Washington, a history of New York, and a history of Spain. George Bancroft made it his lifelong task to write the history of the United States. The first professional American historian, William Hickling Prescott, gave his attention to Spain, and to Spanish exploration and culture, while George Ticknor, his friend and biographer, gave similar attention to Spanish literature.

Some of the most interesting books covered the opening of the west. Thousands of volumes were written by historians, artists, travelers and adventurers.

The Journals of Lewis and Clark told the story of the great scientific exploration conceived by Jefferson, and sponsored by the United States government. Francis Parkman, one of the finest writers ever to be an historian, wrote: "I love the wild not less than the good." Looking first at the land, he described American history in terms of great loss, rather than gain. His careful scholarship uncovered much that had been lost. He recaptured not the innocence which was forever gone, but the adventurous spirit of exploration which thrived on challenge.

Emerson's Leap Into Escapism

Ralph Waldo Emerson was lionized in American letters for six generations because he was able to write so well about the air of hopefulness, which so infused American life and letters during his time. His thought, beautifully composed and unabashedly eclectic, was a leap into escapism by a highly literate and fascinating person. Within himself, Emerson marked the passing of one age into another. Although born in 1803, he was a child of the mechanical age. His interest in individualism and isolation, was in romantic contrast to the thrust of the world about him. Without realizing what was happening, he chose a path of mystical retreat. His work may be seen as a laudable attempt to move away from the materialism all about him, but it is equally true that he offered no answers for those less fortunate than himself. He was a natural ancestor of the new polytheism now so popular.

As minister of Old South Church in Boston, he had a penchant for repeating sermons. He preached the same sermon twenty-seven times, looking for the security of a world in which people might practice what he preached. His refusal to serve the Lord's Supper implies a literalism in theological thinking which was not at all necessary in his time and place. He seems to have mistaken the difference between magic and miracle, between symbol and reality.

As expressed in his transcendentalist philosophy, Emerson's passion for nature was always vaguely sentimental. God Himself became the Over Soul, who had "unobstructed access" to every individual soul. This relationship would manifest itself in nature which was "only the other side of God."

Not one to ignore any sides of truth, and not overly concerned about contradictory conclusions, Emerson in turn was influenced by the Swedenborgians, the Platonists, the Naturalists, the Pantheists, and the Oriental mystics. He seemed to be redefining both God and man—tending to make man divine, and God a natural process. He wrote: "I grow in God. I am only a form of Him. He is the soul of me. I can even with a mountainous aspiring say, I am God."

If Emerson's metaphysics were unhelpful in a period of cultural transformation, his attitude and his methodology were of great value: "But lest I should mislead any . . . let me remind the reader that I am only an experimenter . . . I unsettle all things. No facts are to me sacred; none are profane; I simply experiment, an endless seeker, with no part at my back."

Henry Thoreau was, far more than Emerson, a child of the first culture. His retreat was no more defensible, but his values were more intrinsically his own. He wrote thirty-nine manuscripts, only two of which were published while he was alive. While not deluding himself concerning man's humanity, he took seriously his obligations to the community. The essay "On the Duty of Civil Disobedience," because of its influence on Gandhi and Martin Luther King, has been important for the shaping of twentieth century thought. An ardent abolitionist, who as part of the underground railroad helped slaves to escape, Thoreau personally seceded from the Union in 1845, to protest against a government that tolerated slavery. John Brown's attack at Harper's Ferry made him a man of action.

Walden was his open challenge to the new mechanical age, which deprived man of his sensitivity. Simplicity in writing style and life, were natural for a lover of Greek poetry and oriental wisdom. In *Walden* he wrote: "Most men, even in this comparatively free country, through mere ignorance and mistake, are so occupied with the factitious cares and superfluously coarse labors of life that its finer fruits cannot be plucked by them. Their fingers, from excessive toil, are too clumsy and tremble too much for that. Actually, the laboring man has not leisure for a true integrity day by day; he cannot afford to sustain the manliest relation to men; his labor would be depreciated in the market. *He has no time to be anything but a machine* . . . A stereotyped but unconscious despair is concealed even under what are called the games and amusements of mankind."

He highlighted the conflict which specialization and the hierarchical structure of the mechanical age made inevitable, by asking if men would retain their relative rank and power if they were divested of their clothes. How would people surely know which belonged to the most respected class?

Alone at Walden Pond

In many places throughout his *Journal*, Thoreau endorses pluralism. He recognized conspicuous consumption, before the economists; and the process of depersonalization which prevented men from existing as a community, and freed them from responsibility for others before the sociologists.

He believed that "the mass of men serve the state thus, not as men mainly, but as machines, with their bodies." His life was an embrace of the abundant land, as he attempted to cultivate total awareness in a natural setting. Alone at Walden Pond, his thought exposed the uniformity, the artificiality, and the hollowness of the mechanical age. The attack was given emphasis when he insisted upon a new rebirth rite, demanding that individuals start life over again as those who first came to the virgin land. He especially sought the ethical standards, the close communion with nature, and the sure purpose of the first culture. He found hope in the land, because the land taught the rhythms of life, and held the abundance necessary to right social wrong and provide a foundation for a good life for all.

Writers of the first culture created a literature different in kind, from that which was to follow in the mechanical age. A mass audience of obscure, unknown individuals had not yet been created. All artists of our first culture opened up an abundant land, and discovered a vitality of tradition that Americans still feed upon. They showed life, not only as it was, but as it could be for individuals who had the courage to claim it. The artist had individual freedom of expression. He could go directly to nature for his subjects. In the escape from the predetermined subject matter of church and state as in previous civilizations, color, form, and function came, to the surface.

Sentimental Nothingness

With the mechanical age, the culture of the nation began to change in spirit. In the field of art, the work of Currier and Ives started the decline, in which genre painting lost both its authenticity and its artistic integrity. Beginning in the 1840's, they published three subjects a week for almost fifty years, or more than seven thousand separate pictures. All were color-fully staged and highly sentimental. The people of the mechanical age wanted to remember the old times! Their sales ran into countless millions.

As the industrial revolution proceeded, the natural sweetness was soon condensed into sentimental noth-ingness. It became sentimentalized to the extent of artificial sweetness. Quaint nostalgic themes replaced what had been genuine interpretations of life. When the land was consumed, abused and broken by the mechanical age, culture turned to romance and senti-ment for the masses, and toward elaborate introspec-tion for the educated.

Moving panoramas became popular at mid-century. Oil paintings on endless strips of canvas were unrolled on a stage before audiences. In 1847 John Banvard painted "Life of the Mississippi," claiming to have covered "1200 miles of river on three miles of canvas." He was soon topped by Henry Lewis, who included the entire river from St. Paul to New Orleans—Banvard had covered only the lower half—in sections, which together made a panorama twelve feet high, three times the length of Banvard's. This intro-duced to the art world that common assumption in American life—that the biggest of anything was some-how the best. To portray the largest river of the greatest country on the biggest canvas, was to define success.

As the mechanical age progressed, the American farmer also began to see his sons leave the farm for the factory, and the artist did not follow to interpret life in the factory. Instead he chose to concentrate on the luxurious drawing rooms of the newly rich. And when the artist left the life stream of America, he abandoned his own cultural heritage. Homer and Eakins alone continued in the flow.

It is interesting to note, that the generally recognized decline in furniture began at precisely the time when the craft was becoming an industry. Uniformity came to all forms of furniture in the years after 1830. Each piece had the same form, shape and color. All wood was given the same strain. Fine maple, cheap pine and oak were all stained to look like mahogany. A pseudo-sophistication developed, which insisted that all evidence of function be hidden behind a facade of design, and that everything be elaborately and elegantly "decorated." A machine could give balance, but not rhythm. Accuracy of structure did not bring charm. The dowel replaced the mortise and tenon as even the frame was weakened. The confusion wrought by thousands of books, condensing whole cultures into a few patterns of design, resulted in heavy, clumsy, eclectic combinations.

A consideration of the authors of the period after 1920, which produced William Faulkner, Sinclair Lewis, Willa Cather, Eugene O'Neill, Robert Frost, Theodore Dreiser, Edna St. Vincent Millay, T. S. Eliot, F. Scott Fitzgerald, Thomas Wolfe, Edmund Wilson and Ernest Hemingway, demonstrates their affinity not with the mechanical age, but with the authors discussed earlier in this chapter. Each one was bitterly critical of the mechanical age, and most of them elevated the values inherent in the first culture, and sustained the excellence of those earlier writers.

In this period too, Critic Bernard DeVoto was the

first to note an American tendency to overvalue minor essayists and poets while neglecting more characteristic forms of national experience. He looked to more authentic expressions of culture, the way people talked, what they valued enough to keep in their homes for several generations, what music they loved, and what art they supported.

Urban Center No Cultural Bank

But with the coming of the electronic age all this provincialism, all this isolation from new ideas, from change, from cultural experiences, began reversing itself on a national scale. Today television, radio, records and paperbacks, bring to the largest city and the most isolated village the same cultural input. No longer can the urban center form a cultural bank, carefully limiting deposits and withdrawals, and judging all that happens. There is a common, universal discovery of what is happening. And only recently, when knowledge and intellectual ability have replaced new materials as the most valuable national resource, has the population become mobile again. By the very nature of things, this improved communication should result in an abundance of ideas. Communication will allow the rapid circulation and implementation of new ideas. Those closest to the problems will have access to the accumulated experience of the world's peoples to solve those problems.

In the twentieth century there has evolved an interpretation of art as entirely self-sufficient. This was a brilliant response to the mechanical tendency of endlessly repeating the past, and a futile attempt to escape the brutalizing force of reality. It is epitomized in literature by T. S. Eliot, in painting by Harold Rosenberg, and in music by John Cage. Critics rejected art forms which attempted to communicate anything beyond themselves. They insisted art could not be enthusiastic, could not relate direction to

101

common experience, or interpret meaning.

Expressing prophetic riddles through indirection, and proclaiming through fable, truths which no one can bear to hear, could be an accurate definition of modern art in all its particular forms. Paul Klee, Max Ernest, James Joyce, William Faulkner, and Franz Kafka, worked in a similar fashion. For this reason Poe, since the mid-nineteenth century has been more influential abroad than any other American writer. He was a primary influence upon the movement known as symbolism. Charles Baudelaire translated Poe's work into French, and considered him the first modern artist.

Then there is another interesting sidelight on culture in the electronic age. Many who accept the ethical principles of the first culture, fail to see how they apply to cultural life today. They take for granted that we should feed the hungry or care for the sick. However, there are at least as many people who are utterly lonely and bored with life. Day after day life seems meaningless for them, without purpose or focus. Culture is supremely important, if life is to be happy and full of spirit.

Tyrannized By Critics

Cultural expression is crucial for anyone who seeks a spiritual dimension in life, as basic as the doctrine of stewardship. How will an individual spend his most precious gift, the gift of time? Unless one uses this irreplaceable, unrenewable gift to its fullest, life itself is wasted. The truth of the Biblical phrase, "where your treasure is, there your heart is also," should haunt us every day.

Few would question that the great majority of Americans now fill their time as spectators, letting life slip by as they view television, sporting events, cartoons, comic books, and advertisements. The news, that daily chronicle of the non-happening, has become the greatest time killer of all. The years take on a sameness for all news, all sporting events, all comic books, all television shows, and all advertisements. Tragically, most of our true artists in all cultural fields have been led away from the poetry of the particular and the majesty of the commonplace. Tyrannized by critics who self-consciously define an aristocracy of taste, artists maintain their roots and their creativity only with the greatest difficulty.

As we look at the art of the first culture, as expressed in its music, painting, and literature, the reader is asked to compare it with today's cultural expression.

Popular and classical music is by almost any standard, the most important art form in our electronic age. Its styles and rhythms are set by the young. It is a participatory art form, which allows many levels of involvement and appreciation. It has a vitality so often absent from spectator art forms. By its nature, music is the most international of the arts. There are no inhibitions of native language or geographic location. It has the sensuousness of an immediate experience. The colonial home had many of the values of modern architecture including functional design. William Strickland's important volume, "The Public Works of the United States of America" illustrates the great public and private buildings of the first culture. There is an integration between engineering and colonial innovation. Architecture in the first culture was indeed a true extension of the central nervous system of the human beings who called themselves Americans. Could it be that young engineers may be going through the same process in the later years of the twentieth century?

Land the Mysterious Consuming Force

The crisis in culture, so obvious in the value system

currently fashionable, can be met only when the chains of professional criticism are thrown away. For every critic with the clarity and wisdom of an Edmund Wilson, there are thousands who are more comfortable with conventional mediocrity. Especially narrowing is the critical convention of judging a work of art as if it were completely sufficient unto itself. It is not difficult to understand why T. S. Eliot has so many followers. As soon as a critic accepts the claim that art exists only for art's sake, he is relieved of the responsibility of communication in terms of the history and culture of mankind. By responding only to an isolated happening, he creates an absolute relativism which finally destroys all cultural values and may yet destroy artistic integrity.

It was Mark Twain's contempt for such a culture that established his preference "for experience over sensibility, truth over elegance, simplicity over sophistication, (and) artlessness over art."

Only when American values reflect the richness of the abundant land do they seem authentic. To be sure image is always an ideal, never a reality. The land was never virgin soil in a cultural sense. The innocence was always an attitude of the people, not inherent in the land. As Poe and Melville knew, the land itself had a mysterious, consuming force, able to mold and shape its inhabitants. As long as the struggle was with the land, devoid of massive mechanization and artificial urban concentration, it produced an authentic culture, far from perfect, but uniquely American.

What 4 Is It All About?

God Quietly Retired

Many scholars believe that America, with most of the western world, has moved into a post-religious era. God as a problem solver who answers questions at the boundaries of life—illness, death, guilt, and failure—has been quietly retired. They believe that life is being lived on a pragmatic, empirical, existential level of awareness, with religious dimensions ignored. The only difficulty here is that the problems continue to exist. The emptiness continues to expand.

And in order to see if God has indeed been quietly retired in the years since the nation's beginnings, it might be well to examine first of all the theology of America's early years, its place in the lives of the people, and how that theology and its influence has changed and modified since the first culture.

For one thing it may be that American culture has never been significantly influenced by institutional religion. Only at the very beginning, in the time of settlement, did religious structures motivate cultural expression to any great extent. At the time of the Revolution fewer than ten percent of the American people were church members. Even less were participants in the life of the institution.

America has always been, essentially, a secular culture. The founding fathers were not influenced by institutional religion, preferring Deism and other continental philosophies. Religious pluralism became a way of life in America, which became the first nation without an official religion. At the same time, however, Americans have always dealt profoundly with spiritual questions. Spiritual values have influenced artists such as Hawthorne, Emerson, Thoreau, Poe, Copley and Melville, even though their interest was in meanings, not institutional form.

And while institutional religion has been without fundamental influence, the Biblical tradition was a part of the character of many of the early settlers. Puritans and Pilgrims in New England, Catholics in Maryland, Anglicans in Virginia, Dutch Reformed in New York, Quakers in Pennsylvania, and the Independents of Rhode Island, joined to give their common book to America. Almost every group of settlers came as part of a pilgrimage, claiming a new life in the new world. Many had been persecuted in Europe, and all had been dissatisfied there. Led into the wilderness by legitimate successors of Moses, they intended to follow God's design by finding the Promised Land.

The Puritans were a rebellious people, a fact only recently accepted in history. While they now seem old-fashioned and commonplace, they were then a new, vital, spiritual force. When England refused to be molded by divine design, the Puritans took the analogy of the potter's wheel literally. Now the potter's hand had turned to the clay of America, and a new vessel was to be formed. And all the early settlers had to survive a perilous, two or three month,

3,000 mile sea voyage to reach these shores. Few experiences were more likely to develop a belief in providence or a dependence upon God. Their trial in the wilderness, subject to strange and violent weather patterns, the attacks of Indians and short food supplies, increased their spiritual vocation.

"Scramble For Bigger Farms?"

The first years of settlement were a pilgrimage into the wilderness, for life was hard and earthly compensations few. Death and the future life were heavy on the Puritan mind, because the conditions of this life were dangerous and difficult. Journals and diaries were filled with references to the hereafter. Sermons consistently concentrated on the trials of life. However, with the coming of prosperity this emphasis persisted only as a minority concern. Governor Bradford recorded that within seven years the Pilgrims were neglecting both individual spiritual life, and the church, in a "scramble for bigger farms and a higher standard of living." Popularizations of the excesses of that period usually portray America's first settlers as religious fanatics. Yet, the great majority were already occupied with secular concerns. And their success, while it brought wealth, destroyed their spiritual power, for the wealth of the abundant land soon shaped popular belief with far more authority than any theology.

Only a few principles of Puritan theology had a lasting effect upon American civilization, but these principles have remained at the center of spiritual life. Before the Puritans it was generally agreed that the most holy and pious were monks and hermits who withdrew from the world into monasteries, to protect themselves from temptation and corruption—with their first concern the nurturing of their own spiritual life. The Puritans on the other hand believed that man serves God more effectively in the world, than in spiritual retreat.

Every vocation, every work effort, was a divine calling, as surely as the sacred ministry. The Puritans believe that individuals, if they are to serve God, must be in the midst of life. The Kingdom of God must be built in the world. It was the Puritans' idea that the person who retreated from the service of God in the world was irrelevant, not only in society, but before the Father who taught that talents must be spent. This conviction led eventually to lay control and democracy in both church and state.

Puritans also believed firmly that life was a constant battle between God and Satan, with Christians fighting as Christ's soldiers against the forces of evil. And this belief not only brought the necessary discipline, courage and optimism needed to turn the wilderness into the abundant land. It also shaped American character for generations. Although secular images would replace the spiritual ones, the value Americans place on victory, success and competition, has roots in a popular misunderstanding of Puritan theology. Although often naive and simplistic, the Puritan preachers did lift up a basic dichotomy at the center of life, between good and evil. A person stood either for Christ or against Him. The good was Biblically defined and clearly understood. All who stood against that good were evil. There was no place for neutrals in Puritanism.

It is ironically interesting that the sophisticated intellectuals, who in the early years of this century accepted a philosophical doctrine of progress, a behavioristic psychology, and optimism in politics, have generally changed their minds. Hitler's inferno, the two world wars, Korea and Vietnam, the agony of worldwide depression and starvation, and totalitarianism in all its forms, make talk of the demonic less ridiculous than it once appeared.

Puritan Theology Was Good News

Puritanism was the most rational and logical of all

theologies of that time. It presented nature as God's gift to be used in the service of man. It saw reason as man's tool, with which he could open and understand both God's revelation and natural truth. This heritage gave Americans the pragmatic tradition basic to problem solving, and the technical tools necessary for the exploitation of natural resources.

The Puritans sought a personal communion with God. Communion with God replaced all institutional concerns for them. And this was no abstract doctrine, but a necessity. There were few institutions to worry about. Puritans knew themselves as sinners, but their emphasis was not on the sin. Because confidence was not in the self, but in the goodness and saving grace of God, Puritan theology was good news.

The Puritans thought of themselves as being a "peculiar people" with a providential destiny. When the abundant land of America offered up its wealth, it was taken as evidence of divine blessing, and as confirmation of their mission. Although spiritual foundations for material success soon sank into the unconscious, the tacit optimistic assumption about existence, so typically American, had its beginning there. Even today, it is commonplace for Americans to look to spiritual recources when life is difficult.

As a movement toward direct communion with God, without the necessity of any external aids, Puritans were antagonistic to institutionalism, especially the formalism of the Roman Catholic Church of the 16th and 17th centuries. Theologically centered in the congregation, Puritanism denied any need for a priest-mediator, or for a sacerdotal system. The eternal presence completely saturated the secular environment. Symbols of the divine spirit were found everywhere.

Life, for the Puritan, was structured under the authority of the Bible, especially its teaching that man was estranged from God, needing forgiveness, redemption and salvation. This heritage not only continues to feed the popular faith of millions of evangelicals, but is the foundation for the most characteristic of all American personality traits: the experience of guilt in the midst of abundance. The dependence of secular society on psychiatry and psychoanalysis, and the extraordinary preoccupation of all Americans with guilt feelings about sex, can be traced to Puritan doctrine. Puritans searched their Bible and took it whole. But at the same time, again and again they changed their minds when they found new truth in the Biblical word. They were open to see a new way to do things, to reappraise, because they were Biblical. They recognized its authority, thus they were constantly testing life and opinion by the Biblical word.

The Puritans valued the covenant God made with Abraham, believing that it had been extended from the children of Abraham to the remnant of God's people, who were now settling the new world. This covenant was a gracious undertaking of God, who, for the blessing and benefit of mankind, entered into a special relationship with those who would commit themselves to a common pilgrimage with Him. Faith as a communal experience necessarily involved one with others. If all men have a common God, then they all are brothers, responsible for one another. The covenant eliminated any division between a secular and a spiritual world. A heavy emphasis on the Old Testament and Hebrew culture, cemented spiritual and secular concerns together. The tendency of American religions to be socially involved in the wider secular community, was rooted in Puritan theology. The Covenant involved men with God and with one another.

The Puritan No Militant Predestinarian

Old Testament imagery abounds in all aspects of the first culture. And although sin has been clothed in

110

psychological and sociological terms, it has remained an ever present theme for cultural expression in every American generation. From Hawthorne to Faulkner to Updike, our best artists have plumbed the depths of man's estrangement for meaning. Later fundamentalism was to move in to corrupt the Puritan heritage. This was a narrow, literal view of the Bible and of life, which claims to adhere to the fundamentals of faith, and judges all who disagree as fallen sinners. It redefined sin as unacceptable personal behavior, and gave the doctrine of sin to the revivalist as a weapon. But man's inhumanity to man remains one of the most fundamental of cultural themes.

The moralistic legalism, in which the Puritan is only partially responsible but always blamed, is much more a product of 19th century fundamentalism. Moralistic legalism is the attitude that good behavior can be simplistically defined and legislated, and one group therefore tries to force all to accept its morals and live according to its principles.

Another historical misunderstanding has been the identification of the Puritan as a militant predestinarian. Predestination is the doctrine that all are forced by their created or inherent character, to act as they do. Good and evil are thus predetermined. This crucial Calvinistic doctrine was not stressed by the New England Puritans. Historian Samuel Eliot Morrison, after reading hundreds of sermons, found they believed that salvation was within the reach of everyone who made an effort. God helped those who helped themselves. He concluded that a fatalistic emphasis was completely wanting in their view of religion. The New England Puritans believed rather in the assurance of victory based on a trust in God.

The covenantal origin of the local church gave autonomy to each congregation, and the congregation had superiority over the clergy. This was not necessarily an inheritance from Puritan theology. The clergy tried to maintain superiority, but in town after town in early America, they were overruled by the "will of the saints." Even Cotton Mather was unable to maintain control. Jonathan Edwards himself was turned out of his parish. The village culture became secular because early American laymen read the Bible for themselves, discovering that it applied to all areas of life.

Augustinian Heritage

Augustine, not Calvin, was the theological father of American Puritans. His teaching that "He who abides in love, abides in God, and God abides in him" laid the groundwork for the positive contribution of American theology. Whenever American religion has been judgmental, moralistic or sectarian, it has moved away from its Augustinian heritage. American Puritans, following Ramaean logic, also embraced all forms of science as the means of a more profound knowledge of God's creation.

Throughout the period of the first culture, the church performed a multiplicity of functions. It was the educational and recreational arm of the community. The worship service was the medium of communication for the village. The Preacher shaped the standards of Puritan life, performing the same functions that teachers, novelists, journalists, movie and television personalities do today. Puritans "made" history during the week, and heard it explained on the Sabbath. The sermon was always more than one hour in length. Parishioners often took extensive notes, later discussing the message at the farmer's nooning, at home or in school.

The Bible, the foundation for all efforts at education, was read daily in almost every home. Those boys and girls who learned to read, began with the scriptures. Every student who went beyond elementary school had a reading knowledge of both Biblical languages, Hebrew and Greek, and a real command of

Biblical content. Few communities in history have been more influenced by Jewish culture and spiritual teachings. Hebrew, a language stripped of adjectives and adverbs, is only able to deal with concepts and abstractions in concrete illustrations, using active verbs. With roots in natural physical activity, it gave voice to the natural imagery of an abundant land, possessing emotional depth and great moral strength.

Seriousness to the Sabbath

Franz Kafka once said of Picasso: "He registers the deformities which have not yet penetrated our consciousness." This is a nearly perfect description of colonial preaching. The divines were interested in recording the pervasiveness of sin in the natural world. They brought seriousness to the Sabbath, and intensity to the society.

Children of their time—the Age of Enlightenment, the Age of Reason—Puritans gave first importance to the scholarship of their clergy. At age 12, Cotton Mather could read Virgil, Homer, and the New Testament in their original languages. In his lifetime he wrote in seven languages, and published works in Spanish, French and Iroquois. Three hundred of his volumes were published. And his scholarship was not atypical for the people of the Book. The first culture was modeled in great part on Hebrew civilization, and on the culture of the twelve tribes of Israel. This heritage was filtered by both the practical necessities of settlement, and as a logical extension of the Age of Reason.

From the outset, some settlers of course were not comfortable in such a tight, patterned system. Roger Williams resisted the standards of conformity and hypocrisy, which were often demanded by the Puritan establishment. Another, William Penn, came to America to establish a "free colony for all mankind that will come hither," one which emphasized honesty and tolerance in faith.

In 1705, Solomon Stoddard decided to reject the essence of the covenant theology—that church membership be limited to those who would give a profession of their faith. When he offered the Lord's Supper to all citizens of the village, instead of limiting it to those who offered evidence of conversion, he initiated what was to become a gradual erosion of Puritan influence. Although many have interpreted his innovation as "democratic," it was really the opposite. Instead, his action brought the entire village officially and directly under his autocratic control. "The Elders," he wrote, "are to rule the Church, and therefore not to be over-ruled by the Brethren." He brought to the frontier, Governor John Winthrop's belief that the people should be seen and not heard.

Stoddard's grandson, Jonathan Edwards, succeeded him as minister in Northampton in 1726. Not only was he the most able and original theologian in American history, but he profoundly influenced the content of the first culture. A child of his time, Edwards preached the tenets of Calvinism, but he did not approach the fanaticism so commonly ascribed to him. In contrast to his grandfather, he insisted that an individual must have personally experienced conversion to be admitted to church membership and communion. He abandoned the "half-way" covenant, and with it made the classic American doctrine of the separation of church and state inevitable. He preached a new congregationalism, which accepted democratic principles and established the local church as an autonomous unit.

Edwards was, in fact, a liberalizing force in his time. He had little of the fundamentalist's spirit, requiring only a simple basic commitment for church membership—a sincere hope in Christ. The full text of the shortest of the four forms of the covenant acceptable to Edwards was: "I hope I do truly find heart to give myself to God, according to the tenor of the covenant of grace which was sealed in my baptism, and to walk in a way of that obedience to all the commandments of God, so long as I live."

It was the English philosopher, John Locke, in his *An Essay Concerning Human Understanding,* who was the decisive influence on Edward's life. As he read Locke, Edwards realized that "God's way . . . is indirection, which is the only way because speaking the unspeakable is impossible . . . man can acquire the materials of reason and knowledge solely through experience . . . (God) does not rend the fabric of nature and break the connection between experience and behavior. The universe is all of a piece, and on it God works upon man through the daily shock of sensation . . ."

A Spiritual Basis For a Secular Culture

Although this now seems to be simply common sense, it was at the time crucially important. It gave meaning to the experience of village life, by recasting Puritanism in "the idiom of empirical psychology." For the village culture, this meant that every activity and every experience could have meaning. Significance was not limited just to some philosophical or theological abstraction. Every part of a person's experience was valid and valuable. Suddenly, any dichotomy between the sacred and the secular did not make sense. Edwards had given Americans a spiritual basis for a secular culture. Reinforced by the influence of the frontier, which naturally and persistently weakened the power of traditional institutions such as the church and school, this secular trend became dominant far before the end of the mechanical age.

In addition to the "idealism" which proceeded from his study of Locke, Edwards also developed a "naturalism," which had its roots in Isaac Newton. As the founder of modern physics, Newton brought the new dimension of scientific methodology to his time. Edwards was one of the first to see that theology could not intellectually survive, unless it was integrated with physical reality. Edwards taught that there was a necessary connection between Calvin's law of salvation by faith, and Newton's laws of motion.

In Puritan theology the doctrine of justification by faith had been so intertwined with the doctrine of the covenant, that it became "a right of man" rather than the free gift of God. By his defense of the sovereignty of God, and by his refusal to set reason and revelation against one another, Edwards accomplished the unity of spirit and intellect which gave coherence to the first culture. The forces which had driven the arts out of the church, and prohibited free expression, were temporarily abated. All questions could now be considered, and no part of life was too sacred for human examination.

Choose For Or Against God

In the same period Arminianism was brought by revivalists to America, and it began to infiltrate the sermons. It took its stand on the common sense position that if all men were predestined, then all preaching and Christian service were irrelevant, and the work of the church useless. This belief that men were free to accept or reject salvation, as it was preached by the Baptists and the Methodists on the frontier, was the motivation for evangelicals in America. Basically, they made the claim that in his free will, man has the power to choose for or against God. He cannot save himself, but he can reject salvation.

One minister to embrace Arminianism was Charles Chaucy. In 1782 he published a book entitled *Salvation For All Men—Illustrated and Vindicated As A Scripture Doctrine.* Very quickly thereafter the Unitarian and Universalist movements became strong in New England, and in contrast Edwards was catalogued to history and to his hell-fire and damnation image. All churches embraced the abundance of the land, and courted the good opinion of so successful a people.

Unitarian ministers, Buckminster, Channing, Parker and Dewey were particularly well tuned to the mechanical age as it moved in on the nation. They were sure of the continuing benevolence of God, the natural goodness of man and the unlikelihood of hell. In the early years of the 19th century, there was a new confidence in success sweeping America. Men thought they stood free from sin, exempt from temptation and fall, free to enjoy and conquer. Even if sin happened to be real, liberals believed God would save all. Some were so sure, they called themselves "Universalists."

A Full Blown Transcendentalism

Impressed by the romantic idealism of German philosophy, and only too willing to claim that religion must be exclusively a matter of abstractions, liberal Christians felt the soul had some "inherent power to grasp the truth." Consequently they built a structure which, in the name of objectivity, denied the unity of man. A man's physical and psychological life was not considered nearly as important, as that which transcended the experience of the senses. In the wake of this liberal misunderstanding of the first culture, came a full blown transcendentalism, claiming for the mind all that was innate, original, universal, intuitive and mystical.

Transcendentalism was formulated in reaction to the "great awakening," coinciding with the first stirrings of nationalism following the Revolution. This evangelical awakening had come simultaneously with the citizens becoming aware and excited about a consciousness of themselves as a nation. And the revival caused a permanent cleavage in American

117

thought between religious feeling and human intellect.

The Unitarian liberals accepted the widening gulf, as they followed English philosophy through ever more radical cycles. On the one hand were the rational idealists who depended upon the latest continental philosophy. On the other were the evangelical revivalists who saw revelation as radically distinct from reason.

For the next century, no leader of American religious thought was able to unite the power of evangelical witness with the intellectual respectability of rationalism. This ever widening division separated most spiritually oriented Americans from the emerging intellectual community. The professionalism and vocational specializations of the mechanical age, heightened by this gap and aggravated by sectional differences, gave the industrial East to the liberals, and the advancing frontier of the West to the evangelicals. This division had implications for American politics and education which are still evolving.

Winning The West For Christ

Francis Asbury and the itinerant Methodist preachers joined the Baptists, the Presbyterians, and other sect groups, in the task of winning the West for Christ. Paradoxically, the evangelical movements greatly valued education, and are responsible for a majority of the institutions of higher learning in the United States. Although Methodists consistently advocated social action in the areas of anti-slavery, race relations, temperance, women's rights, and the labor movement, the new fundamentalism—a mixture of mechanical literalism and machine oriented, conformist piety—saw little purpose in uniting religious feeling with secular life. Instead they offered simple choices—Christ or the devil, goodness or sin, faith or infidelity. They insisted that the life of the spirit had little to do with anything except the salvation of immortal souls. Attention was centered on the next world, where God would surely reward or punish through eternity. Those who evangelized the West realized that no Protestant theology—Lutheran or Calvinist—escaped from an abstract intellectualism, which had little to do with the actualities of American life. They discovered the natural wedding between the human potential for evil, and the simple choice of salvation.

This leveling of religious experience came in a weird mixture of individualistic piety and institutionalism. The covenant heritage of the village saw the church as a community of believers, called not by their ability to accommodate one another, but by God. A willingness to accept responsibility for serving all, was replaced by an emphasis on personal salvation. Individuals were "saved," one by one, at revivals, and grouped together with like-minded people in exclusive organizations. This sectarianism made all spiritual experience relative and tended to transform its adherents into judgmental, self-righteous prudes. Religious commitment was leveled either to a vague "American Way of Life" theology, all things for all men, or to a purely emotional religious experience.

In the years following 1850, as a direct result of the mechanical age—for now a person's "religion" and his "faith" were separated from all else in life—fundamentalism, an utterly new religious phenomenon, was born. The groups which embraced its doctrines emphasized a literalist interpretation of the Bible, teaching that each and every word of scripture was directly given by God, and equal in importance to every other word. Fundamentalists preached that damnation awaited all who did not stand with the "we-group" and an extreme limitation of religion to the personal, private areas of life. It also emphasized an aggressive, judgmentalism which demanded that the private, individual morality of the general public conform to the standards of the sect, a subconscious union between outward appearance and ethics, and a new emphasis on nationalistic patriotism. The fundamentalists were so successful in their missionary evangelism—the purpose of the church was not service, but growth—that institutionalism, for the first time in America, became the ruling psychology of all religious groups. Fundamentalism embraced most of the values, and many of the practices, of the mechanical age. The liberal churches made much the same accommodation, but for different reasons.

Emerson, as he glorified both man and nature, so broadly defined God that deity lost any particular meaning. He designated the supreme being as "Over Soul," the "universal essence," "which is beauty, love, wisdom, and power, all in one, present in Nature and throughout Nature." His eclectic philosophy, by implication, denied any unique relevance for Christianity, and encouraged the individualism, which was abroad warping the American character. No less than fundamentalism, the religion of liberalism became an intimately personal experience, which had little to do with secular or community life.

Religious liberals embraced both poles of Emerson's philosophy. Accepting his humanism, they naively trusted in the goodness of man, and in the inevitability of progress. Thus, their commendable social consciousness failed to take into account, either the complexities of the social order, or of a human being. Emerson's naturalism became the foundation for a more sophisticated process philosophy, which had no ethical, and little spiritual, content.

Attack On Puritan Inheritance

The spiritual force of the first culture was lost as religion and became an exercise in good works and good reasoning. The institutional church became one more voluntary association, a group of like-minded individuals who could accommodate one another. Fully as much as fundamentalism, liberalism cast asunder the inclusiveness of the mission of the church, as found in the first culture, in favor of an exclusive society. Furthermore, it embraced many of the cultural habits of the mechanical age: sentimentality, Victorian excess, inevitability of progress, excessive confidence in education, and the acceptance of an institution-centered civilization.

Both liberals and fundamentalists attacked the essentials of the Puritan inheritance. Puritans believed that God was more effectively served in this world, than in spiritual retreat. The liberals, with Emerson, found self-reliance in retreat, meditating on the mystical mysteries of the orient. They strove to be above the battle, basking in the wisdom and the greatness of the mind. Fundamentalists, on the other hand, made a legalism of the Bible, and withdrew from the world, excluding from their ranks all that disagreed. What Emerson did as an individual, fundamentalists did in community, and they both ignored their responsibility for mission and service in the real world.

Puritans taught that life could be understood as a battle between God and Satan. The liberals laughed Satan away in the name of progress and sophistication. The fundamentalists personified Satan, giving him his tail and his horns. Fearful individuals were told they needed the power of an exorcist, if they were to escape the devil. Moving wildly apart from anything in the Bible, preachers caused an unholy terror. While liberals ignored basic ethical problems and the complex agonies of society in the name of a naive optimism, fundamentalists attained the same result by pushing the battle into the dark subconscious of individual human beings.

Puritans taught that life should be structured under the authority of the Bible. The liberals, by adding all the wisdom of the world, lost any standard of truth.

121

Everything was interesting, but everything was relative. There was no word of authority—in ethics, in morals, or in life. The fundamentalists claimed that proof texts taken from any place in the Bible, were as valid and as free from error as the teachings of Christ. This totally ruined the Bible for intelligent people. On the one hand, the Bible became a source for polite conversation and ridicule, and on the other, a weapon of proof by which the believer judges his neighbor.

Slogans Replace Faith

The Puritans taught that personal communion with God and obedience to Him, must replace all institutional concerns. The fundamentalist and the liberal built institutions had measured themselves in terms of numerical success—on how many souls were won and how many people were properly educated. There was a tendency on both sides to let slogans replace faith. The institutional baggage soon became so heavy that it was beyond examination. They measured themselves by counting how many people thought, and lived, in exactly the same manner.

Finally, the Puritan thought, that although there was complete domination by sin in the world, the individual could be confident, because faith was not in the power of self but in the goodness of God. The liberal explained sin away completely, leaving a world where sophisticated, intelligent, and educated individuals conclude that there is no such thing as sin, and yet they have an inescapable and overwhelming feeling of guilt. The fundamentalist, unintentionally twisting the Biblical word, pluralized sin, and used it as a weapon. Biblically, sin described the universal human condition of estrangement from God, a condition corrected only through the saving grace of God. The fundamentalists found so many "sins" in personal behavior and individual habits, that the concept became the method of distinguishing between the good and the bad.

Both the liberal and fundamentalist positions had the effect of removing spiritual considerations from the heart of life. In each of these areas of belief, the Puritan position was lost, and both extremes were weaker because of it. Although more people expressed spiritual needs, the alternatives appeared so weak that the majority of the American people looked elsewhere in confusion.

At the same time both the institutional forms gave up, seemingly without regret, their heritage as patrons of culture. Instead they embraced the worst of vulgar architectural style, the most saccharine forms of sentimental music, and the overly romantic in painting and literature. Both lost relevance in the wider community. The fundamentalist extreme retreated to a stance of individualistic, moralistic piety. The humanist extreme escaped into the equally individualist illusion of a perfect humanity, ever progressing by reason toward a better world. Neither had an adequate Christology, or any message equipped to deal with the new facts of industrialization. While the Fundamentalists had lost the image of Christ as Lord of all life, the liberals, with no conception of Christ as Savior, deified man as the lord of this world. Little did either realize that their action invited institutionalism in its most abhorrent form.

Stripped of spiritual responsibility for their own members, and of ethical responsibility for the community, sect groups turned to their organizations, and measured success exclusively by quantitative standards of self-perpetuation and internal growth. All churches were judged during the mechanical age by the extent of their membership, their property, their wealth, their conversions, and their service to their own members. The liberal church lacked only the measure of conversions. Under such conditions, the secularization of society was hardly noticed. The churches had rapidly retreated to the securities of institutionalism.

Extremes Dominant in Media

Their cultural bankruptcy is adequately portrayed by pathetic attempts to recapture the glories of the past, through the borrowed dignity of Gothic architecture and the ostentation of conspicuous consumption. Ironically, these extremes appealed to middle class citizens, and the church lost contact with the laboring masses—those most oppressed by the new system—and with the leadership community.

Tragically, the extremes of the American religious experience have been dominant in the media—the liberals in books and magazines addressed to the academic community, and the fundamentalists in tracts and on television and radio, addressed to individuals in various forms of personal crisis. Many millions still substantially true to their Judeo-Christian heritage, are ignored.

Many evangelicals in all denominations have escaped both the judgmentalism and the aberrations of fundamentalism. In commitment to Christ and their Biblical roots, they recognize the Lordship of Christ over all actions and possessions, as well as recognition of Him as personal Savior. Evangelicals stand directly in the heritage of the early Puritans.

Many individuals, apart from institutional involvement in religion, have both recognized the spiritual depths of life, and maintained high ethical standards in private and corporate living. Open to tradition, and to new ways of understanding, they are ready to embrace the finest spiritual and intellectual resources available.

The Heritage of Rome

In the midst of the mechanical age, a new element

entered the mainstream of American life—massive and continuous immigration. The vast majority came from Roman Catholic countries, bringing with them a fully developed faith and a richly varied cultural tradition. While at the time of the Revolution, the colonies probably had less than 25,000 Roman Catholics, there were more than a million by the mid 19th century. The Catholic Church preserved the ethnic traditions of the various mother countries, as well as the heritage of Rome. It offered substantial services to the laboring masses. However, while the church gave significantly to literally millions of underprivileged Americans, it tended to develop in them an inbred cultural provincialism. This in itself had the same negative qualities of institutionalism we have seen in other communions. Primarily because of the absurdly bigoted anti-Catholicism which swept through the institutions of middle class Protestantism, Catholics were prevented from entering the mainstream of culture and society. Unconsciously they accelerated the fragmentation and specialization, which would be the hallmarks of the mechanical age. The system of parochial schools, in great part forced upon Catholics by militantly possessive Protestants, tended to create a separate cultural community.

The Catholic Church did maintain a unique life-style for her adherents. Catholics brought with them a rich understanding of oral culture—the Mass, a varied musical and theatrical tradition, and a heritage of peasant communal interdependence. It also brought an advanced appreciation of tactile values—sculpture, stained glass, painting, crucifixes, vestments, and handicrafts. Many Protestants ridiculed Roman Catholic practices before visiting the great Cathedrals of Europe, only to return home acutely aware of the barren and profoundly boring exteriors and interiors of their own places of worship.

Catholics had a theology which related more positively to that of the Puritans and Jonathan Edwards, than to either Emersonian liberalism or fundamentalist piety. Catholics believe in divine providence, in sin and salvation, in Christ as Lord and in the communal church in His body to serve Him on earth, and in the power of the Holy Spirit. Initially all the forces of society worked to prevent understanding and interaction between Catholics and Protestants. In two adjacent warring camps, traditionalists in each community barely spoke, and never cooperated with one another. Both drifted toward the lowest common denominators of their faiths—a deification of the American way of life, and a faith in faith. Especially in the first years of the twentieth century, both Catholics and Protestants were so interested in being identified as Americans, that most religious differences became less visible. Fortunately, now there is a new spirit of cooperation, and a new willingness to appreciate the richness of the common Christian heritage that Catholics and Protestants share.

In the same wave of immigration, Jews first came to America in substantial numbers. A few had enriched the first culture, but Judaism as an institutional religion, was influential in society for the first time during the last years of the 19th century. European Jews, who immigrated to America in the years when the first culture was fading, brought with them, in an authentic and pure form, the fullness of Hebrew culture—the force which filtered through the Puritan experience, and was most influential in forming the first culture. In their religious tradition, social practice, and artistic achievement, many Jews retained these values, unique in their own tradition, and reflected in colonial times. Their minority status made culture precious, and concentrated artistic and creative activity in such a way that its influence went far beyond Judaism.

Greatness of Hebrew Covenant Community

It is no accident that in almost every area of cultural advance, Jews have led in forming the culture of the electronic age. In all the fine arts: painting, sculpture, literature, the cinema, poetry, crafts, drama, television, architecture and commercial design, Jews have made contributions more vital than that of other groups, even though they represent only a small fraction of the total population. Hebrew culture, formed in ancient Israel by the Covenant community, provided roots for all tribal village cultures, colonial or global, and offers the finest available means of meeting the crises now threatening American life.

In light of the intractable realities of the electronic age, the religious alternatives offered by the mechanical age are obviously insufficient. All solutions which pass lightly over the unpleasant complexities of life, or ignore its spiritual dimensions, are doomed to failure. The attainment of happiness cannot be separated from the attainment of truth.

Many religious liberals have exchanged their optimistic innocence for a paralyzing absorption with the sins of the society. Once they denied the existence of evil, proclaimed unfettered progress, and taught the natural goodness of man. Now, with a magnificent lack of intellectual consistency, they give all their time to social concerns and political activity.

Christ Bottled and Labeled

Fundamentalists, tragically misunderstanding the Bible they revere and the Christ they proclaim as savior, now give all their energies to institutional advance and proclamations of self-righteousness. Like spiritual gypsies they spend life seeking purely religious experiences, while neglecting Christ's mission in the world. They seem to have Christ securely bottled and labeled, for a we-group to use in support of the mores, the taste and the patriotism of the middle class.

It is astonishing how both groups molded religion into the same sociological form: a mixture of meetings, services, building funds, charities, picnics, clubs and public statements. For most Americans, the rough edges of the liberal and fundamentalist heritages have been rubbed away, forming the American Way of Life.

What can Americans retrieve from the religious past that would be workable today?

What can they reach for in the past, to get rid of the current spiritual malaise that now affects the nation?

Well, for one thing a viable faith for the electronic age must see with Augustine both the complexity and the unity of life. Humility and concern have become the primary virtues. Questions have become more important than answers, since change is now central to all of life, even to spiritual understanding. The boundaries of spirit will not be contained within any nation or state, or any creedal statement, because such artificial boundaries tend to destroy truth.

A free society must have religious and cultural diversity without the destruction of the spiritual depth of the culture. Every expression of faith must energetically present its best contribution. At the same time it must search for an attitude of humility and sacrifical service, in the knowledge that all religions are subject to intellectual error and historical contingency. Tolerance and conviction complement each other well, only when truth is found apart from self. Since no one possesses all of the truth, it would be foolish for anyone to claim official monopoly or governmental sanction for a particular point of view.

This same attitude gives freedom to all to seek out the spiritual strength that all need.

Such a religious context allows a renewal of faith in God, expressed in works of compassion and benevolence. A balanced religion furnishes spiritual vitality as well as intellectual depth. It brings into life dimensions of mystery, justice, love, understanding and delight. That's what the nation needs to plow spiritually into this promised land of the electronic age.

Clings Fast to Previous Period

This book has summarized the current problems of the United States, using as a perspective, the experience of the first American culture. As we arrive in the electronic age, it is worth looking at these values and attitudes to see what they have for us that is valid today. The first culture asked questions now ignored, and accepted standards now rejected. At the same time its track record is pretty impressive, considering that on those standards this country was given its foundations.

As the mechanical age becomes the electronic age, and Americans move into the middle of their second revolution, the period summarized here, has a peculiar fascination. While the mechanical age was forming, the first culture, in response to the challenge of mechanization, revealed itself with clarity and majesty. In a similar way, in response to the advances of the electronic age, the mechanical culture is trying to dominate contemporary art forms. Popular culture always clings fast to the previous period, while real artists predict the future and transform the present. An attempt has been made to force fit the cultural current of the mechanical age—its novels, drama, music, educational methods, religion, politics—into the media of the electronic age—television, movies, records, tape, radio and jet transportation. But at the same time, conforming to the new awareness of the young, this content is subtly undergoing inevitable change, much of which we are tempted to damn—and for good reason.

Yet the only thing more dangerous than change, would be no change at all. The first culture would have been equally exhausted and bankrupt, if it had solidified into a frozen status quo, rejecting the industrial and scientific revolutions. No hothouse of sheltered loyalties could have kept the first culture intact. And now that some of the values of that culture are being honestly reclaimed, Americans may have to struggle with the temptation to treat them as beautiful fossils—as if they were sentimental nothings from a bygone era. They are not. The great things, the real values about the first culture are vital, living forces. They need transplanting in the Promised Land of this electronic age.

No Naive Greening of America

This book has been the chronicling of the basic values underlying these changes from the first culture, through the mechanical age, and now into the electronic age. It has revealed no naive greening of America. The land has been raped, but the values and attitudes which first claimed it, can today be reclaimed. If Americans awaken to a new involvement with their heritage, for the first time in more than a century, they will see life as just beginning. In perspective, the current crises are little more than a challenge to the mechanical way of doing things.

Maybe Victor Hugo's tale *Ninety-Three* symbolically capsules our situation more clearly than anything else. A great ship is caught in a roaring, raging storm. Suddenly the terrified crew hears a loud crashing sound down in the hold. A cannon they are carrying as cargo has broken loose. It is smashing into the ship's sides with every roll of the sea. It is far more dangerous than the storm, for soon that which is in the belly of the ship may burst into the sea. The corruption loose within, will pound and pound until the fabric is destroyed. So it has been with American culture. It has created its own mechanical fetters. Now they are being thrown off, as the abundant land is appreciated again. The precious heritage of American geography is again a living, breathing thing which can realistically support that early attitude of confidence and hope when it is combined with the resources made available by electronic technology.

And when other vistas of tomorrow dawn, those same values of our early cultural heritage will be as important in accepting even greater changes than necessary in the transition from the mechanical to the electronic age. By the time space exploration reaches Jupiter, we may have made contact with intelligent life, and a cultural heritage as unlike ours as that of prehistoric man. Change will become much more certain in human experience than death itself. Yet, amid all the change, the model of the first culture will have unique relevance, for its basic value structure remains authentic in an abundant land.

The New Day

"The only assurance of our nation's safety," wrote Abraham Lincoln, "is to lay our foundations in morality and religion." This book suggests that the technology of the electronic age permits a recapture of those foundations if we have the will. We may have seen the weakening, and even the destruction of America's spiritual foundations, but current confusion is eloquent testimony to the vital importance of ethical and spiritual values. Without them even hope in the future is seriously eroded. Many parents fear that their children's lives will be much harder than their own. A general feeling that the quality of life is slipping has snowballed into a national malaise.

Some traditional American virtues have become vulgar as they have lost their spiritual roots:

. American good will expressed as a sense of

responsibility for others is projected around the world: in Vietnam, Korea and the Dominican Republic.

American images of success, requiring aggressive and competitive accomplishment, are projected throughout the nation in terms of the worst wave of violent crime in the world's history. While the hungry in other lands remain resigned and timid, watching food pass by on the streets, our style of success make crime and injustice inevitable.

The discipline and scientific innovation which produced the production records of American business, leaves pollution and ecological disaster in its wake.

The complete saturation of electronic media has so raised the consciousness of the people, that a feeling of perpetual dissatisfaction with one's own lot in life pervades.

Increasing realization of equality of opportunity inevitably elicits demands for equality in results, an utterly unattainable goal in a free society.

It should be no surprise that economic abundance enhances qualities of wastefulness, selfishness and frustration. It does so because it always arrives at a time when the custodial care and protection of possessions requires a strain and effort inconsistent with the joy the possessions bring. At the same time that wants are thought of constantly as needs, physical abundance eventually corrupts unless it points to a spiritual goal.

American Dreams Come True

The fact is that all of the original material objectives, the original American dreams, have actually been realized in the electronic age. The parents of children born in the depression—our current leaders—

have seen all their dreams for material success satisfied. Yet they and their children remain unfulfilled. The sons and daughters are caught up in the frustrations and inadequacies of material success. They have enough possessions, so at the same time they are impatient with quantative goals, especially as they are realized today. This generation of young adults has not yet reached any consensus on new goals or dreams. This book suggests that the material goals of the mechanical age destroyed the more authentic spiritual goals of the first culture—goals that are especially viable in an electronic age.

Very recent studies trace a change toward intentionality among the young. A *Fortune* poll shows that "the work ethic is still alive among young Americans." Their desire for spiritual values has led them to search with more vigor and less discernment than any previous generation. Some are into Eastern religions, yoga, the occult, witchcraft, astrology and various forms of mysticism. Amid this confusing search for values and self—sometimes perilously naive, irrational, and selfish—most young people have made a commitment to truth beyond materialism. They are often people centered and spirit oriented. Many are looking at vocations as a "calling" in which one can find self-realization in the effort to create a better self and a better world. The idea that a person lacking a college education should feel inferior is almost gone. Many are also finding physical work an escape from both the obscure and the abstract, a way of coming to terms with oneself.

There seems to be a new possibility evolving in the electronic age—an authentic union of traditional and modern values. There has been a new appreciation of the values of the first culture: integrity, inner discipline, craftsmanship, pride, prudence, rationality and satisfaction in work. There is also a willingness to use these values from the American past in a practical way. There is almost an impelling push in the lifestyle of the electronic age, which involves spontaneity, personal autonomy, relaxed interpersonal relationships, mobility, and openness to new ideas and new experiences.

This appreciation, plus a willingness to practical application, provides a new vision. It brings together the values inherent in the first culture, and the attitudes made possible by the electronic age. The movement of accommodation is already under way. Americans willing to cultivate a non-judgmental attitude of openness, are already beginning to understand the necessary linkage between discipline and freedom, between responsibility and success. The unity of life made possible by joining modern technology and traditional values in this electronic age, may yet renew this abundant land—make Americans see it as the Promised Land it indeed is.

Suggestions
for
FurtherReading

Charles A. Beard, *An Economic Interpretation of the Constitution of the United States* (Macmillan, 1935).

Ray Allen Billington, *Western Expansion* (Macmillan, 1962).

Arthur C. Bining, *The Rise of American Economic Life* (Charles Scribner's, 1953).

Daniel J. Boorstin, All works, especially *The Americans,* 3 vols. (Random House) and *The Image* (Atheneum, 1962).

Hector St. John Crevecoeur, *Letters From An American Farmer* (Doubleday, 1782).

Catherine Fennelly, *Life in an Old New England Village* (Thomas Y. Crowell Co., 1969).

S. G. Goodrich, *Recollections of a Life Time,* 2 vols. (Miller, Burr & Hyde, 1856).

Greeley, Case, Howland, et.al., *The Great Industries of the United States* (Burr & Hyde, 1871).

Talbot Hamlin, *Greek Revival Architecture in America* (Oxford, 1944).

Edward C. Kirkland, *A History of American Life* (F. S. Crofts & Co., 1944).

John A. Kouwenkoven, *Made in America* (Doubleday, 1962).

Perry Miller, all books, especially, *Errand into the Wilderness* (Harvard, 1956).

    The Life of the Mind in America (Harcourt, Brace & World, 1965).

    From Colony to Province (Harvard, 1953).

    The New England Mind (Harvard, 1939).

    The Trancendentalists (Harvard, 1950).

Samuel Eliot Morison, *The Intellectual Life of Colonial New England* (New York University Press, 1956).

Hugh Morrison, *Early American Architecture* (Oxford, 1952).

Frank Luther Mott, *A History of American Magazines,* Vol. 1 (Harvard, 1957).

Vernon L. Parrington, *Main Currents in American Thought,* 2 vols. (Harcourt, Brace, 1927).

Merrill D. Peterson, *Thomas Jefferson* (Oxford, 1970).

The Jefferson Image in the American Mind (1960).

George Santayana, *Character and Opinion in the United States* (George Braziller, 1955).

Arthur M. Schlesinger, Jr., *The Age of Jackson* (Little, Brown & Co., 1945).

Spiller, Thorp, Johnson, Camby, & Ludwig, eds. *Literary History of the United States,* 3rd Ed. (Macmillan, 1969).

Robert Francis Seybolt, *The Public Schools of Colonial Boston* (Harvard, 1935).

George Rogers Taylor, *The Turner Thesis* (D. C. Heath & Co., 1956).

Alexis de Tocqueville, *Democracy in America,* 2 vols. (Alfred A. Knopf, 1945).

Mrs. Francis Trollope, *Domestic Manners of Americans* (Alfred A. Knopf, 1949).

Frederick Jackson Turner, *Frontier & Section* (Prentice-Hall, 1961).

Rise of the New West (Macmillan, 1962).

The Frontier in American History, 1920 (Holt, Reinhart & Winston).

Van Doren, Trent, Erskine, & Sherman, eds., *The Cambridge History of American Literature,* 3 vols. (G. P. Putnam's Sons, 1937).

Edmund Wilson, all works, especially *Patriotic Gore* (Oxford, 1962).

The Shock of Recognition (Farrar, Strauss and Giroux, 1956).

Classics and Commercials (Farrar, Strauss and Giroux).

The Works of Poe, Thoreau, Melville, Hawthorne, Emerson, Irving, Bancroft, & Parkman

Index

A

Adams, Henry, 94
Adams, John, 95
Adams, John Quincy, 57
Allston, Washington, 84
"Ambitious Guest, The," 90
American West, 18-20
Architecture, 69-73
Arminianism, 116
Art, 62-65, 72-73, 75-76,
    80-85, 99-100
Asbury, Francis, 118
Audubon, James John, 85
Augustine, 112-113

B

Badger, Joseph, 79
Balloon Hoax, The, 88
Bancroft, George, 23, 96
Banvard, John, 99
Baptists, 116-118
Baudelaire, Charles, 102
Bernstein, Leonard, 29
Bible, 26, 112-113
Bierstadt, Albert, 81
Billings, William, 68
Bingham, George Caleb, 84
Blackburn, Joseph, 79
Blythe, David, 84
Bradford, William, 94
Brown, John, 97
Bryant, William, 23
Bunyan, Paul, 63
Business, 46, 47

C

Cage, John, 101
Calvin, John, 112, 116
Camus, Albert, 87
Capitalism, 27, 31, 40, 41,
    43, 45, 46

Cather, Willa, 100
Catlin, George, 84
Chambers, Thomas, 81
Chandler, Winthrop, 80
Channing, William E., 20, 117
Chauncy, Charles, 116
Church, Frederick, 81
Coates, E. C., 81
Cole, Thomas, 81
Columbus, Christopher, 95
Constitution, 57
Cooper, James Fenimore, 86
Copley, John Singleton, 78-79, 106
Crockett, Davy, 63
Cromwell, Oliver, 54
Currier and Ives 99

D

Declaration of Independence, 55, 56
De Voto, Bernard, 100
Dostoevsky, Fyodor, 87
Doughty, Thomas, 81
Dreiser, Theodore, 100
Durand, Asher B., 81

E

Earl, Ralph, 77
Eastman, Seth, 81
Edison, Thomas, 29
Edwards, Jonathan, 94, 114
Electronic Age, 12, 42, 45, 129-131
Eliot, T. S., 100, 101, 104
Emerson, Ralph Waldo, 23, 82,
    95-97, 106, 120
Ernst, Max, 102
Eustace, Edward, 67

F

Family, 15, 23, 35, 37
Farming, 36, 37, 38, 39
Faulkner, William, 86, 100, 102

Feke, Robert, 79
Fitzgerald, F. Scott, 100
Foster, Stephen, 69
Franklin, Benjamin, 59, 68, 94
Frost, Robert, 100
Fuller, Margaret, 89
Fulton, Robert, 22
Fundamentalism, 119-124, 127-129
Furniture, 71

G

Gandhi, Mahatama, 97
Gehot, Jean, 68
Gerry, Eldridge, 55
God, 60-62, 105, 106, 107-116, 119
Goodyear, Charles, 20
Gramm, W. Philip, 30, 31
Greenfield Village,
     Dearborn, Michigan, 80

H

Hamilton, Alexander, 55, 59
Hawthorne, Nathaniel, 23, 82, 86,
     88-92, 106
Hawthorne and His Moses, 89
Hemingway, Ernest, 100
Hesse, Herman, 87
Hicks, Edward, 83
Hitler, Adolph, 108
Hotels, 34-35
House of Seven Gables, 91
Howe, Elias, 20
Hugo, Victor, 130
Huntington, Daniel, 81

I

Ibsen, Hendrick, 87
Innes, George, 82
Integrity, 15, 39-41, 44, 47, 51
Irving, Washington, 86, 95
*Israel Potter—Fifty
     Years of Exile,* 94
Ives, Charles, 68

J

Jacob Fowle, 79
Jefferson, Thomas, 53, 55,
     57, 59, 94
Jesus, 60-61, 108-110, 114-115,
     118, 123-125, 127-128

*Journals of Lewis
     and Clark,* 95
Joyce, James, 86, 102
Judaism, 126-127

K

Kafka, Franz, 86, 87, 102, 113
King, Martin Luther, 97
Klee, Paul, 102

L

Land, Fitz Hugh, 81
Lewis, Henry, 99
Lewis, Sinclair, 100
Liberals, 120-123, 127
Liberty, 56
Lincoln, Abraham, 131
Literature (American), 86-98
Locke, John, 52, 55, 115
Longfellow, Henry Wadsworth, 63, 89

M

Malraux, Andre, 28, 40
Mather, Cotton, 94, 112-113
Mechanical Age, 32, 100-101, 129-131
Mellonta Tauta, 88
Melville, Herman, 82, 86, 89,
     92-95, 104, 106
Methodists, 116-118
Millay, Edna St. Vincent, 100
Minister's Black Veil, The, 90
Moby Dick, 92-94
Monck Mason, 88
Morality, 49
Morrison, Samuel Eliot, 111
Morse, Samuel F. B., 78
Mount, William Sidney, 84
Music, 66, 67

N

Nader, Ralph, 46
National resources, 15, 25, 27,
     47, 50
Newton, Isaac, 115, 116
Niebuhr, Reinhold, 21

O

Old Sturbridge Village, 80
O'Neill, Eugene, 100
"On the Duty of Civil Disobedience," 97

P

Paine, Thomas, 57, 59, 95
Parker, Theodore, 117
Parkman, Francis, 95
Peale, Charles Willson, 79
Penn, William, 113
Picasso, 113
Pierre, 94
Pinckney, Charles, 53
Poe, Edgar Allan, 86-88,
    102, 104, 106
Porter, Rufus, 80
Prescott, William Hickling, 95
"Public Works of the United
    States of America, The," 103
Puritans, 26, 40, 54-56, 59,
    64-65, 106-110, 115-116,
    120-122

R

Racial injustice, 24
Randolf, Edmund, 55
Religion, 119
Revere, Paul, 74
Revolutionary War, 21, 77, 106
Roman Catholic Church,
    109-110, 124-126
Rondell, Frederick, 81
Rosenberg, Harold, 101
Rossiter, T. P., 81

S

*Salvation for all Men:
    Illustrated and Vindicated*, 116
Scarlet Letter, The, 90
Schoenberg, Arnold, 68
Shelbourne Village, Vermont, 80
Sherman, Roger, 55
Mrs. Sigourney, 86
Smibert, John, 79
Social Darwinism, 42
Some Words With a Mummy, 88
Stoddard, Solomon, 114
Stravinsky, Igor, 68
Strickland, William, 103

Stuart, Gilbert, 79
Success Ethic, 50, 51, 59, 61,
    62, 97, 98
Sully, Thomas, 79

T

Television, 28, 44, 103,
    124, 129
Thoreau, Henry, 63, 82, 89,
    97-99, 106
Ticknor, George, 95
Transcendentalism, 117
Trunbull, John, 79
Turner, Frederick Jackson, 18
Twain, Mark, 104
Twice Told Tales, 90

U

Unitarians, 116-117
Universalism, 116
*Unparalleled Adventure of
    One Hans Pfaal, The*, 88

V

Vietnam, 24, 132
Vonnegut, Kurt, 65

W

Walden, 97
Washington, George, 55, 57, 59, 66, 95
Watts, Isaac, 66
Wesley, John and Charles, 66
West, Benjamin, 77-78
Western America, 52
Whitman, Walt, 23
Whitney, Eli, 20, 22
Williams, Roger, 113
Williamsburg, Virginia, 80
Willis, Nathaniel Parker, 86
Willson, Mary Ann, 80
Wilson, Edmund, 100, 104
Winthrop, John, 94, 114
Wolfe, Thomas, 100
Woolson, E., 80
Work Ethic, 15, 17-20, 45,
    51, 72-74, 98, 133-134

139